*There is never a problem
that does not include a gift for you.
You seek out problems
because you need their gifts.*

Richard Bach, Illusions

Jasmin Schober-Howorka, born in 1962, is a trained life coach and counselor who for years has led seminars and training groups for „Integrative Family Constellation." Moreover, she also regulary offers open doors evenings to learn more about her work. Individual constellations are also possible in her office in Graz, Austria. Remote constellations can also gladly be done via email.

You may contact the author at:

Jasmin Schober-Howorka
St. Bartholomä 106
A-8113 St. Oswald, Austria
Tel: +43 664 112 7514
Email: jasmin@ich-bin.com
Event calendar at: www.ich-bin.com
Distance training groups: www.family-constellations.net
Facebook: www.facebook.com/jasmin.familyconstellations
Skype: jasminevelin
Twitter: https://twitter.com/JasminSchober
Youtube: http://www.youtube.com/JasminSchoberHoworka

With her integrative family constellation, the author has been able to blaze new trails in constellation therapy. She enriches the reader with images from both this and previous lives with the gift of her intuitive perception. This book offers new resolution statements to resolve entaglements from previous lives, promises from partnerships, contracts of the soul, and oaths and vows. For better clarification, the reader has a wide range of current case studies dealing with topics like partnership, sexuality, family, finances, and career. This new method of remote constellation offers advisors as well as clients new possibilities to overcome both spatial and temporal limitations in the course of constellation work.

Jasmin Schober - Howorka

Family Constellation and Past Lives

with newly-developed methods and resolution statements

An exciting manual with many case studies

Integrative Family Constellation according to J. Schober-Howorka®

All mandalas designed by Ms. Agathe Petignat.
You may admire her artwork in color at www.mandalas.ch

All rights to distribute, including by radio, television,
photomechanical reproduction,
all sound recording media and reproduction in extracts reserved.

Cover design: Gerwin Maria Glöckner
Cover-Photo: http://de.fotolia.com/id/36760325
Cielo e mare - texture retro © lapas77 #36760325

Copyright © 2012
Jasmin Schober-Howorka
www.family-constellations.net

Printed: www.lulu.com
ISBN: 978-1-300-21180-8

the German Version „Familienaufstellung und frühere Leben" is published by
© 2007 Schirner Verlag, Darmstadt, Germany
5th Edition 2012 © Schirner Verlag

TABLE OF CONTENTS

Acknowledgements 9
Introduction 11

INTEGRATIVE FAMILY CONSTELLATION 13
Previous lives 17
Karma 19
Partnerships and previous lives 21

INTEGRATIVE FAMILY CONSTELLATION AND
PREVIOUS LIVES 23
Our ancestors as a reflection of our dissociated personality facets 23
Destined entanglements or causal correlations 23
Shadow facets 24
Good and evil 24
Victim and perpetrator – fear of one's own power and force 25
Awareness of unity 26
Self-responsibility 27
Possession by the deceased 28
The masculine and feminine divine channel 31

NEW METHODS OF INTEGRATIVE FAMILY CONSTELLATION 32
Remote constellation 32
– Working with pillows 32
– Working with blocks 32
– Working with a charted family genogram 32
– Remote constellation procedure 33
– Kinesiologic testing 33
Unborn siblings from the mother's womb and their meaning 35
Intuition and inner images in my work 37
New resolution statements for release from promises, oaths, vows and
contracts of the soul from present and former lives 41
Contracts of the soul 47
Additional helpful resolution statements 49
Curses 53

INABILITY TO HAVE CHILDREN 55
Possible causes from the ancestral system for an inability to have children .. 55
Possible causes from previous lives for an inability to have children 56

Frequent questions regarding physical symptoms and the inability to have children 56

THE INNER CHILD IN US 59
What is the inner child? 59
What does work with the inner child entail? 59
Constellating the inner child 60
The inner child and previous lives 61

CASE STUDIES FROM MY PRACTICE 62
Case 1   "I'm afraid of my clients" – Balancing guilt with atonement 62
Case 2   "Dear twin brother, I miss you!" –
Candace's growth on her left kidney 66
Case 3   Finding your own path in life –
freedom from slavery and external control 68
Case 4   "You abandoned me" – the path to your own life energy............70
Case 5   A lack of income –
competition with my father in a previous life 72
Case 6   "My partner is unable to open up to me" –
Fear of losing power 74
Case 7   Guilt and atonement through rheumatic pain –
Denied love for oneself 76
Case 8   "I want to develop creatively" –
lacking sense of personal identity 78
Case 9   "I can't orgasm" – a vow of chastity 81
Case 10   Being free for your own family –
assuming a father's power and strength 83
Case 11   Love that wasn't allowed to be – Russian melancholy 85
Case 12   My husband won't take responsibility for himself 87
Case 13   "Careful during sex!" –fear of accepting the masculine 89
Case 14 A "I'm invisible" – the brother who died in infancy 90
Case 14 B The masculine threat – perpetrator and victim 91
Case 15   Doubts about fatherhood – an insecure identity 92
Case 16   My sister's jealousy – unequal inheritance 94
Case 17   Physical pain as an offset for guilt 96
Case 18   "I feel guilty – I failed!" – a separation 98
Case 19   "I'll protect you, mama!" –
No one else will care for my mother 99
Case 20   "We can't get close to one another" – forbidden love 102
Case 21   "I have to sacrifice my life for the relationship" –
the harem wife in servitude 103

Case 22	"My fear of my boss" – old feelings of guilt towards my father	104
Case 23	Longing for and rejection of Jesus	106
Case 24	"Things can't go well for me" – blocked joy for life	107
Case 25	Pregnancy and sexuality – the lethal threat	109

Cases dealing with an unfulfilled wish for children

Case 26	"Dear great-grandmother, I honor the loss of your four children" – Unfulfilled wish for children	111
Case 27	"I'm responsible for your death" – a previous life as a babysitter	112
Case 28	Hormone deficiency – feelings of guilt from a previous life	114
Case 29	Folic acid deficiency – forbidden love as a nun	115

ANIMAL CONSTELLATIONS ... 117

| Case 30 | My dog's enteritis – anger towards my husband | 117 |

HEALING IMAGES ... 121

Good resolutions in a constellation ... 121
Former lives as a blockade in a constellation ... 121
A partial resolution as a good resolution ... 121
We can only resolve what our soul reveals ... 121
Effect of a healing image ... 123

QUESTIONS AND ANSWERS ... 125

Afterword ... 129
Glossary ... 131
Bibliography ... 135

ACKNOWLEDGEMENTS

First I'd like to thank my parents, whom I deeply love and who enabled me to have the experiences which accompanied my personal journey. By dealing with my own problems over the years, I developed the ability to help others. My husband, Robert, deserves my gratitude for standing by me as a coach, editor and driving force while writing this book. I'd also like to express special gratitude to my clients, who have graciously allowed me to share their case studies. This book wouldn't' have been possible without them. I'd also like to thank Heidi Bacher, who helped me write and inspired me with good ideas.

INTRODUCTION

My personal journey

Even as a child, I would paint trees from the top downwards. They were very full with many branches, but the trunk was narrow and there were hardly any roots to speak of. For a long time, I drifted through my life in the same way. I found my first physical foothold in massage; by touching other people, I began to understand myself better. I fondly worked with body masses that I'd never sensed myself; my own body weight was more like that of a feather, blown hither and thither by the winds of life. 15 moves, diverse jobs and even my relationships couldn't withstand my quest for constant change very long. It certainly wasn't a boring life I led; I was steadily focused on personal development. When I was 19, my father died in a car accident. We were very close and up to this point I had oriented my life according to his wishes, out of a dependent love that desired to make him happy and never disappoint him. Then he disappointed me by suddenly leaving me alone, and my "pseudo-life" began to crumble. As an acclimated bank employee with a white blouse and blue pleated skirt, I quit my then secure job and found my first "alternative" boyfriend with long hair and an earring in his ear. My fashion statement included flowery clothing from the '70s. That was my first revolution. My father's death was a great shock and very painful, but his gift to me was room to set off on my own path of self-discovery, transboundary experiences and quest for the meaning of life. It was one of those wounds, which later proved golden. Experiencing survival, developing strength, growing up and awakening! At the same time, I was searching for my father, for God and for myself - I wanted to arrive at a place of security and love. Although I received much love from my partners, I had difficulty accepting it. At the point when I was loved most, I left. It wasn't really meant for me – that's what my constantly searching spirit had decided – and I had to confront the thing I longed for most and simultaneously feared: love. To long for love is one thing; to accept it is quite another. I was able to liberate myself from a longing for death, the desire to follow my father to the grave, through family constellation. I was able to release myself from many external entanglements and created a foundation of received ancestral support and roots under my feet. Today, I can focus on my own life and have become open for a partnership that is able to succeed.

Insights into previous lives gave me the possibility to recognize burdensome correlations from yesterday and today, to release myself from old pacts, oaths and vows that are no longer beneficial to my current life. With a combination of genealogy and dissolving karmic entanglements from previous lives, I have been able to experience a lot of healing in my life. I'd like to share the steps to the solution I've developed with this book, so that you can also experience release from old burdens and enjoy an untroubled life.

The true is the whole.

But the whole is only an essence that can be complete through its own development.

Georg Wilhelm Friedrich Hegel,
Die Phänomenologie des Geistes (Phenomenology of the Mind)

INTEGRATIVE FAMILY CONSTELLATION

What is integrative family constellation?
We are all on a quest for our true selves! This journey leads us from a duality, in which everything appears separate, back to unity. There, we are connected once again with everything, safe and complete. On this path, we collect everything which we were previously unable to grant entry into our hearts; we integrate it. It is usually the shadowy parts which cause fear and which we'd rather project onto others than identify ourselves with.

Many paths to family constellation have already been trodden. "Integrative family constellation" by J. Schober-Howorka®, which I established, is an extended form of constellation work, which developed from our "extended consciousness." Until recently it was our ancestors, which we intensively worked with in our constellation in order to release ourselves from identifications and entanglements. In my current constellation work, images from previous lives serve to release our souls. In this way, we are freed from the causal hindrances which influence our current life. Childhood injuries want to be healed to make room in our hearts for our parents and our partner. We can dissolve assumed doctrines and anchor ourselves with a positive self-perception.

Integrative family constellation is the taking in of what we need to arrive at a holistic solution.

We live in a fast-paced world that constantly offers us new and improved methods to further develop ourselves. The classical constellation models from Virginia Satir (family therapist) and Bert Hellinger (psychologist and theologian) provide a wonderful framework that confers order and system on the concept of family. I am deeply grateful to both of them for being able to work with this methodology and to enrich them with my newly developed methods.

If the systemic, logical consultation model previously sufficed, today it is increasingly the feminine, intuitive thinking of our right cerebral hemisphere that must be integrated. We should once again place more trust in this inner perception, even if we cannot explain it intellectually. I see a wide range of inner images in the constellation process. I have learned to trust these images and they have always led me to the solution. I would never have been able to achieve this with logical reasoning alone. Especially regarding external constellations, I am directed to my inner images in order to crystallize a solid overview. One year ago, I couldn't have imagined the possibility of a constellation without the presence of my clients; today it's completely normal for me. Two years ago, I was foretold that in the future I would draw family constellations only on paper – including the solution. Back then, I thought that this would be possible only at a much later date. Today, I primarily work with this form of constellation.

> **We are currently living in a period of amazing possibilities for healing and development of ourselves, towards our whole, towards this fantastic, divine core of our beings.**

Rebirth:

The ultimate reason

for its existence is that

our consciousness as a being

of pure light and cognition

must have originated from a previous impulse

for light and cognition.

Consciousness cannot originate from matter.

Dalai Lama XIV, The Logic of Love

PREVIOUS LIVES

Working with previous lives
Belief in previous lives, which is prevalent in Buddhism and Hinduism, has become more widespread in our western culture in recent decades. Many people believe that they have lived previously. I was personally convinced when I read it for the first time, but was not especially interested in who and what I once was. I thought that it would distract me too much from this life. Over the course of healing therapies, though, various lives were depicted that had causal connections to my current life. I was very impressed with the descriptions of my previous lives, since several of them had repeated in my current life. It helped me to understand which learning experiences I had not yet completed and therefore carried with me into this life. To consider yourself possessing one single life often provides too little context. From a single life perspective, one could say that life is unjust for some unfortunate souls, in that they must suffer while others lay claim to happiness. If one contemplates current life in the context of various previous lives, the sum results in a puzzle that leads to a cohesive whole.

Examples
Isabella M. identifies with the feelings of her grandmother, who was raped in World War II by three Russians. Isabella carries her feelings of powerlessness, shame and abuse. She unconsciously senses the male threat that her grandmother experienced. During testing, it was revealed that Isabella was one of the Russians who had raped her grandmother at that time. Here you can see a balance of guilt (for more information, see Case 14 B The masculine threat – perpetrator and victim). When working with original family constellations, I often discover that many of the women entangled in the victim scenarios of their ancestors were actually the offenders from those previous times.

Exact information from previous lives
Most of the time, I only see images from previous lives that correspond to my present life. Dates, places and names don't play a role. Knowing exactly who he or she was and where and at which time these lives took place can divert the person from the real issues at hand. It is sufficient to recognize just the images necessary to find a good solution. Those who are interested in exact dates from previous lives should explore regression therapy.

If there are future lives,
then the quality of those next lives
depends on the quality of this life.
If you live responsibly now,
this will have positive effects on the next life.
Anger, adherence, etc.
leads us to an unfavorable lifestyle
and this leads to damaging consequences in the future.

Dalai Lama XIV, The Logic of Love

KARMA

What is karma?
In general, karma is understood to be the law of cause and effect. In simpler terms: "You reap what you sow." We carry positive and negative experiences from various lives in a memory bank. Sometimes we were the 'good' people and other times the 'bad' ones, since both are part of the learning process of polarity on this earth. Karma is often associated with guilt, in the sense that there is something that must be made right. I believe that in reality there is no guilt, but rather personally chosen learning experiences. Each of us has a conscience that feels unwell when we've done something bad to other people and induces an urge for balance and redress.

Karma in the ancestral family
We don't even have to look back into previous lives. Even in our own ancestral families, there is an unconscious codex which states that those born after must atone for their ancestors' wrongdoings, which are remembered in their sad destinies. The Bible says, "You will bear the sins of your fathers for seven generations." I can confirm this from my working experiences.

Example
If the grandfather's fiancée was rejected because she didn't correspond to the family's social status, then this love could not succeed. Later, the next generation or even several generations may experience a similar fate and, in an act of solidarity with the grandfather, not allow their love to succeed. Only after the grandfather's then-fiancée is honored, respected and receives an esteemed place in the family system is a resolution possible, allowing love to flow again.

Karma from former lives
We bring the issues that we want to resolve and heal from previous lives into this life. We have concluded contracts of the soul with various people in order to embark on specific learning experiences with them. In relationships, the term karma is of particular importance. Have you seen a relationship where you just couldn't understand why such a kind man got together with such a dislikable woman, or why this nice lady is together with such an absolute macho man?
You think the whole situation is really unfair, that people deserve something better. From a one-life perspective, something like this seems unfair and haphazard. You might not understand why your sister received the entire inheritance and you yourself were excluded (see Case 16) or why one person suffers great physical pain while others enjoy perfect health (see Case 17). However, if you take the perspective from previous lives into consideration, then everything suddenly makes sense. Then we recognize a causal correlation between all of the

occurrences in our life/lives. Here, the principle of cause and effect or the urge for balance and redress becomes clear.

> **Our life is not a punishment placed on us by others! We ourselves have chosen this destiny. We, as the playwrights, stand behind the most difficult experiences in our lives.**

PARTNERSHIPS AND PREVIOUS LIVES

Many of our partners in this life we do not meet for the first time. You surely know the situation when you feel immediately familiar with a stranger, as if you've already known them forever. We've very often had several lives with one another, which in no sense were purely positive and harmonious. One presumes that souls that feel very connected are there to confront especially difficult learning experiences together. Most of us have done mutually bad things that can burden our relationships still today.

When we speak of karmic relationships, we are speaking of those partnerships that appear unavoidable. One can never be free of the other before the agreed lesson has been learned. In such relationships, the term karma means balancing negative causes from previous lives. One must do something good for the other this time around.

Examples

A client came to me and explained that her husband suddenly came up with the absurd idea that she wanted to poison him. Fearfully he checked each dish before drinking or eating from it. The constellation showed that she had definitely poisoned him in a previous life in order to succeed him as heiress. His mistrust was therefore based on an unconscious memory that old fears had awakened in him. His wife was at her wit's end, because he wouldn't let go of his suspicions. She couldn't bring herself to leave him; he was very sick and required her care. It became apparent that her nurturing care for him was to balance out the old karma. A karmic relationship can manifest itself in such a way that one can treat the other very badly and still won't be left by their partner. Or, to take another example, when someone marries the same partner twice, even though the marriage was a huge fiasco. People on the outside simply cannot comprehend such situations. They can't understand why the one won't leave the other for a better life. As the well-known author Hermann Mayer so aptly said in the title of one of his books, "Everyone gets the partner they deserve, whether they want to or not." From a karmic perspective, this sounds very plausible.

When we meet a partner from a previous life anew in this life, a pleasant, familiar memory rises up in us in the beginning to help us to make positive contact. Once we get past the honeymoon phase and remove our rose-colored spectacles, then we see other sides of our personalities, which for the most part prove to be a challenge for us. It is here that the mutual learning experience or karmic lesson begins, which we must master. Integrative family constellation helps us to recognize basic interconnections in our current relationship dynamics, solve karmic issues and in doing so encounter our partner more freely.

Identify yourself. Those who can identify themselves often find more than a single person in themselves

Daniel Czepko von Reigersfeld
monodistic sapientium

INTEGRATIVE FAMILY CONSTELLATION AND PREVIOUS LIVES

Our ancestors as a reflection of our dissociated personality facets

Even our ancestors, with whom we are entangled, embody personality facets that we have not yet integrated. That's why it's not the bad ancestors that possess us or wish us ill because they led difficult lives. No, we borrow their destinies for ourselves in order to serve us in our own development.

> **It is always ourselves whom we confront!**
>
> **A universal law states that we can only be connected with something that has something to do with us; otherwise blows of fate, possessions, curses or other burdens cannot do any harm to us.**

Destined entanglements or causal correlations

When we look at family dynamics without the background of previous lives, many entanglements seem random. Clients ask me again and again, "Why do I carry this burden and not my sister?" For a long time, I didn't really have an answer to this question. I thought that many things serve us as learning experiences. We must remember all of the difficult fates that were not resolved in our ancestral family. Only after I was shown images from previous lives in my constellations did a clear correlation between cause and effect emerge. Through many cases that I observed in my practical experience, I became aware that we carry destinies like unfulfilled love, financial problems, illnesses, depression and much more from previous lives in order to resolve them this time around.

We choose our own parents so that we can gain the learning experiences we require. They are without doubt the most important people for us, since we carry their genetic legacy and all its associated personality facets in ourselves. Some of these we readily accept and others we adamantly refuse: "Mom, Dad, I'll never be like you!" To us, they may reflect facets of hard-heartedness, sternness or dominance, from which we dissociated ourselves due to experiences in an earlier incarnation.

> **Through our entanglement with our ancestors, we have the chance in this life to resolve old karma from several previous incarnations.**

Shadow facets

It's not the good sides of our ancestors which we reject; much more it is the shadow facets (such as misuse of power, sternness, violence, oppression, adultery, jealousy, illness, an unhappy life, etc) that we have trouble dealing with. What abused child wants to take his perpetrator to heart? If you were oppressed or sexually or emotionally abused, those are the characteristics that you would avoid at all costs. Any woman whose father was unfaithful could not bear to suffer a fate similar to her mother's. Nevertheless she often ends up with someone just like her father! We push away these shadow facets, from which we have dissociated ourselves, to a place where we can continue to observe and fight our concept of the enemy. In order to come to terms with these undesirable shadow facets, we need the courage to ask, "Why did this happen particularly to me? What is the lesson behind this that I must learn? Which causes have I put into motion for myself?"

> **When I come to the realization that I choose every experience in this life for myself, both the best and the worst, then I can take responsibility for myself and change my situation!**

Good and evil

Here on earth, we can learn from the polarity of good and evil. Religious institutions in Western culture actively discourage us from granting evil a space within ourselves. That's why we have the devil, who is our scapegoat for everything. We can act on only one side of this polarity, namely that of the good, otherwise we will go straight to hell. Nonetheless, we cannot escape our shadow facets. Just as in Goethe's Faust, "It is one force, which always wants the good and always creates the evil." We carry these shadows in us and they want to be accepted and integrated. Very often in my constellations I confront these conveyed values from the Western church, which prevent us from experiencing our entirety. Nothing is so bad that it can't be taken to heart! Through this work, I have discovered that ultimately everything happens through love and that the worst experiences are the most valuable, since they make us vulnerable and, ultimately, human.

And yet evil is necessary for good,

just as material for an idea

and darkness for light.

Simone de Beauvoir, The Second Sext

Regarding the church just discussed, I would like to emphasize here that I do not imply a judgment of these institutions! The church is a bearer of belief in God and goodness in people. I regard these institutions as an important promoter of inner values that provides many people with a footing, community and faith. However, wherever there is light, you will also find shadows. These shadow facets - vows of chastity in the Catholic church, for instance, which are broken often enough and whose consequences we read daily in the media - are signs of humanity. Such signs show us that even bearers of very high values are ultimately only human beings with natural needs, which demand recognition. Most of us have served the church in one way or another in previous lives. Just like everything else, it is a part of our own creation. We have independently adopted all of our belief systems, vows, notions of heaven and hell and other moral concepts. Thus, we also have the possibility to turn graciously away from those moral concepts, which no longer serve us today (see Case 24).

Victim and perpetrator – fear of one's own power and force

Victim and perpetrator – fear of one's own power and force
It is difficult to continually play the victim, because it requires giving up our own power and projecting it elsewhere. In doing so, we also relinquish responsibility for ourselves, in that we make others responsible for everything and seek external culprits for our own lives. No healing can take place with this approach, since I have no power to make any changes. The others have the power; they are the bad ones, the perpetrators, the culprits; those are the facets that I want nothing to do with. Fears often stem from previous lives, in which we misused our power and force or were tortured and killed for our power and knowledge. It is logical that in subsequent lives we prefer the role of the victim, in order to avoid similar dangers. It is probable that everyone on this planet has already lived many lives as perpetrator and victim. Most of us have already lived and suffered through the most abysmal experiences!

*I seek unity in everything,
so that with it I may permeate everything*

Confucius

AWARENESS OF UNITY

Today's chairos, in the Age of Aquarius, is a time of "freedom, equality and brotherhood". The central point is equality and a desire for unity instead of separateness. The European Union is just one example of borders that are continuously receding, cultures that are mixing. A consciousness of unconditional love is waiting to manifest itself here on earth. Each of us wants this unconditional love; we all desire to be accepted as we are, but we have to develop it within ourselves first. Only then are we able to instill this love in others. This unconditionality comprises everything - both the good and bad facets, just as one imagines a loving god who loves regardless of judgment.

SELF-RESPONSIBILITY

Integrative family constellations, which extend beyond our ancestors and reveal the causal correlations from earlier times, can show us a larger picture of ourselves. Everything that we find so difficult to accept in this life is a part of us that we lived to excess in previous lives and dissociated from ourselves. The external is a reflection of the internal! Everything that we see around us is always just ourselves.

Once we assume responsibility for our lives and see ourselves not as "destiny's pawns", but rather "creators of our reality", then we are one big step closer to God. We have been granted free will. The decision is ours to make!

POSSESSION BY THE DECEASED

Possession means that the soul of a deceased person slips into the body of a living person. Very often, this energetic possession leads to a loss of vitality in the person affected. It can also lead to confusion and disorientation, since one is not able to sense things for oneself. The reasons for possession are varied. It could be that the soul of a deceased person is straying because it is not aware that it is already dead or can't find its way to the next level. This is especially true for those who perished suddenly, like victims of war. They are so traumatized by shock that they are not aware that they have already passed away. Some people are so connected to material things that they cannot disengage themselves from them after their death. They live for long periods of time as metaphysical energy in their original homes and seek contact with their loved ones.

Possession by ancestors
There are different types of possession. Those I experience most often in my work are possessions by ancestors. In this case, one not only identifies with a deceased ancestor, but is also energetically possessed by him. The reason for this is often feelings of guilt. After someone prematurely passes away, it can be hard to take one's own place in life, and the result is an unconscious transferal of one's bodily energy field to the deceased. Sometimes the reason is one's own longing for death, that one would rather be in the afterlife, and thereby leaves his place in life vacant for the deceased. As soon as one has determined which deceased ancestor the problems are connected to, then such possessions can be resolved.

Karmic possession
There are other possessions related to living people. Some people relinquish their energy field to someone else, and allow their own life energy to be transferred to this person. They subsequently feel tired and empty, a very similar feeling to being possessed by the deceased. In both cases, one's own energy is surrendered.

A practical example
As we were building our house, I conversed for a long period of time with one of the assistants at the construction site. That evening, I noticed how my bodily energy kept decreasing until I went to bed fully exhausted. The next morning, I didn't feel rested at all; I was still completely exhausted. Through kinesiologic testing, I recognized the following images from a previous life: I see myself as the mother of a son, who was the man employed as an assistant in building our home. In that previous life, I led a very eccentric existence and didn't want the responsibility of caring for my son, so I gave him up to an orphanage.

Consequences for my current life
These subconscious feelings of guilt towards my previous son caused me to give him the majority of my life energy. At the moment I became aware of this entanglement, I assumed responsibility for my former mistake as a mother and gave him back responsibility for his life. Today he is no longer my son and is responsible for himself. As soon as I came up with the solution, it was as if the possession simply blew away and I regained my energy. I see it as a karmic balancing of guilt, which luckily lasted only a short time.

Possession through working with energy
A healer once said to me, "I don't like energy healings – you go in alone and come out as a party of three!" During healing session, my energy has been tapped or I have come away with the energetic burdens of the healer or their ancestral possessions. At this point I must emphasize that I subconsciously assented to this. Sometimes I had to disentangle myself from this respective person or I was confronted with an insufficient boundary placement. I also know about possessions from constellation seminars. Those who have difficulty setting boundaries often find it hard to completely let go of an assumed role as representatives. If one serves as a representative for a deceased person, then this can lead to an energetic possession. One takes this energy home and often needs external help to get rid of it. These kinds of possessions during constellations only occur if one cannot sufficiently step back from the role and neglects other purification rituals after a constellation. Since I went through this exasperating experience often enough during my training, it's a priority for me to ensure appropriate cleansing after representing various roles in my constellation work. When it happens despite precautions, it always has to do with oneself. Weakness in setting boundaries is a sign that one not centered in life and easily relinquishes or sacrifices one's energy to others. Those bearing many entanglements with the deceased in their own family system will have a difficult time in separating themselves from the deceased when assuming roles. One takes them home energetically in order to confront them. This is a sign that a similar theme of one's own needs to be resolved! Possession is not threatening. It can be quickly and easily resolved.

*We cannot see God,
but we see the divine everywhere*

Friedrich Schlegel, Lucinde

THE MASCULINE AND FEMININE DIVINE CHANNEL

Just as everything here on earth is present in ourselves as a polar duality (father and mother, day and night, heaven and earth), the avenue to our divine essence also consists of two poles: the feminine and masculine divine channels in ourselves.

The image was conveyed to us with the birth of Jesus Christ – God came as a man! That's why many people consciously or subconsciously picture God as an old man with a long beard or Jesus Christ as God's only son. The Father, Son and Holy Spirit are a trinity lacking a feminine dimension! Even today, it is impossible for women to become priests in the Catholic Church. Since we have been carrying these Christian impressions with us for centuries, it requires intense effort to transform our image of God into a balance of the feminine and masculine. If we fail to do so, women must bear a subconscious doctrine: "As a woman, I am not worthy of having God flow through me." From my experience, I know that even men feel an unconscious guilt revolving around this imbalance. The consequence of this is that many men, in solidarity with women, cannot truly devote themselves to this image of God. Injustices are therefore not only atoned for in our ancestral systems, but also collectively balanced.

With regard to the Bible verses passed down to us, literature has provided us with many new approaches to the existence of a goddess. Mary Magdalene is depicted as the incarnate feminine pole of Jesus time and time again. It also ought to be added that she was most likely not a prostitute (see Bibliography).

A practical example demonstrates the consequences for our current life.
See Case 23: Longing for and rejection of Jesus

NEW METHODS OF INTEGRATIVE FAMILY CONSTELLATION

REMOTE CONSTELLATION

I was inspired to attempt remote constellation by a friend and colleague of mine, Rosa Ehgartner. She encouraged me to remotely do constellation work with a client of hers. At first, I had my doubts as to whether constellation could work without the presence of the client. However, the positive feedback removed all my reservations.

Selecting the medium

I first chose the object I would use for the remote constellation. Pillows, building blocks, chess figures, chairs, stones, shells, and much more can be used. The best thing to do is to choose a medium with which you like to work. For me, working with pillows and blocks turned out to be the best medium.

Working with pillows
The advantage of working with pillows is that I can sit on them, making it easier to physically slip into the role of each representative. When doing constellations in a group, I sometimes use chairs or pillows in order to avoid placing unnecessary strain on a representative contending with difficult roles or deceased persons. Even if you have too few representatives, other constellation objects can be very helpful! The size, shape and pattern of the pillows are an important tool for what is then expressed.

Working with blocks
I use blocks when I want to create a clear view of a system, in other words when I want to capture a "meta level". I can thereby see the whole picture at a glance, which is more difficult with larger objects or group constellations with people. When working with blocks, I feel mentally connected with the various roles and receive images that lead me to a solution. Equally with blocks, the selection of colors, sizes and shapes are important and communicate important attributes.

Working with a charted family genogram
Very often, I work with neither pillows nor blocks, but create a healing resolution directly with the family genogram, which is drawn on a piece of paper that I place in front of me. It contains an overview of one's genealogy up to five generations. I use kinesiologic testing to determine which ancestors are entangled or identify with my client and determine the necessary steps for resolution.

Remote constellation procedure

I see myself as a representative for my client(s) and intuitively choose pillows or blocks for the representatives and place them according to my inner perceptions. When working with pillows, I sit on these and slip into my client's role in order to sense how they feel. What needs to be changed in the situation? From the practitioner's perspective, most dynamics are easy to recognize. In order to create the whole picture, I place myself in other representatives' positions - it can be helpful to confirm what you've experienced from various positions. When working with blocks, I intuitively create the image, but mentally slip into the various roles. Even with this method, I can recognize all necessary steps to the healing resolution. Kinesiologic testing is thereby an important aid in assessing my inner perception.

Words are powerful - they bring about solutions

As soon as I've identified an entanglement in the constellation, I speak the necessary resolution statements from my client's position and then test to see if these bring about absolution. I subsequently inform my client of each phrase that works well. The client can then speak these phrases at home and direct them to the person with whom the entanglements are to be resolved. I usually recommend repeating the resolution statements on three different days within a week so that they can solidify. Speaking these phrases is liberating and leads the client to assume responsibility for the solution to his situation.

Kinesiologic testing

Trusting in my images is good, but examining them is better! I repeatedly assess the accuracy of my intuition with kinesiologic testing by means of the arm length test. This muscle testing method provides me with the security of trusting my perceptions. Of many various testing methods, the arm length test has been the most reliable for me over the last fifteen years.

Client identification with remote constellation

It is important that my clients participate in the entire constellation process. Only after they are familiar with the images and feelings experienced can they truly identify with them and feel understood. By speaking the resolution statements, the client strengthens his personal participation in the process.

Advantages of remote constellations

A major advantage of my new method of remote constellation is that one can overcome spatial and temporal distances. I increasingly receive calls from clients in other countries for whom it is difficult to visit me personally. Modern times are often too fast-paced! In urgent cases, arranging individual or group appointments takes too long. With remote constellations, I can react more quickly to the needs of my client. What I especially value in remote constellations is that I can slip into all of the roles and determine the entire situation from my own perspective. It brings out the best in me, since I have no one else to depend on. The depth of my inner images helps me to efficiently find solutions.

UNBORN SIBLINGS FROM THE MOTHER'S WOMB AND THEIR MEANING

Through his work on regression, psychologist Dr. Norbert Mayer discovered that 70-80% of humans were not alone in their mother's womb. Many of us once had between one and five siblings. However, these disappear within the first three weeks of pregnancy and are therefore not recognized. "Arguably, there is no way that we can have conscious memories from the initial days of this prenatal phase. It has, however, been proven that in a state of deep relaxation, humans can remember back to the time of their conception. They can see precisely what happened to them and around them. Dr. Mayer's clients have described the loss of their siblings in the womb as very painful and, in some cases, traumatic. They initially feel an inner closeness and togetherness, followed by sudden separation upon the death of the siblings (literary reference to Der Kainkomplex [The Cain Complex], by Dr. Norbert Mayer). In my constellations, I observe this strong connection and the associated pain of separation again and again. Often, my clients have a feeling of guilt towards their unborn siblings. They believe that they displaced their siblings in the womb and feel responsible for their deaths. I call these unborn siblings an "emotional escort service," because they come into our lives for a short while and then quickly leave again. I see an especially strong connection if someone had only one unborn sibling. These twin siblings form a common unit; without the other one just doesn't feel complete. Many of my clients have confirmed a feeling that someone is missing in their lives, that they don't feel whole. It is common to have a karmic connection between siblings from previous lives. Very often, our unborn siblings were previously our partners. One must resolve old promises in order to free oneself for a partnership in this life.

Through kinesiologic testing, I know very quickly if there were unborn siblings from multiple fertilizations. In most cases it is necessary to perform constellation work in order to resolve entanglements. For a practical example of this, see Case 2: "Dear twin brother, I miss you!" – Candace's growth on her left kidney

For humans, the biggest imaginable struggle against their own instinct and taste lies in disbelief. This entails forever foregoing the joys of imagination, all propensities for the miraculous.

Ferdinando Galiani, Thoughts and Observations

INTUITION AND INNER IMAGES IN MY WORK

All humans possess a certain degree of intuitive inner perception, which one cannot account for though reason alone. Some have premonitions and others have a sixth sense during pivotal situations in their lives. Since our society is highly scientifically oriented and requires attestable proof for everything, we act primarily with our left cerebral hemisphere, which represents the masculine, logical and mathematical side of us. However, we also have a right cerebral hemisphere, which has a feminine, pictorial and intuitive approach to the world. We must train this side more so that we can learn to trust it. For far too long, it has been dismissed and neglected. Many new forms of therapy correspond to our feminine cerebral hemisphere, such as color therapy, singing bowl massage, channeling, reading, aromatherapy, etc. I often experience that many of my clients have a wide range of inner images, but do not trust these because they cannot immediately classify them using logic and reason. If we are open to these images, though, they lead us like a puzzle to a larger context, which then also becomes understandable.

Intuitive perception during constellation work
Over many years in my work, I have learned to trust my intuition and inner images. Only by opening yourself to "that which is" can a healing resolution appear. Classical family constellation is primarily viewed as a systemic work that brings order to our ancestral background and offers those who were excluded a good place once again. That is also the basis of my work. Furthermore, I allow my soul the freedom of revealing things of importance to me. Very often, I deal with straining family secrets that require an enormous amount of intuition in order to bring them light.

I kinesiologically test much of what the representative or I perceive during constellation for accuracy. It is good to check images, since you can make mistakes or insert your own interpretations.

> **A constellation is a reflection of the constellator. Most constellations can be comprehended with logic. However, there are some in which everything that appears cannot be immediately allocated. Therein lies the art of recognizing the latent wisdom of the soul, which only reveals itself to our understanding at a later point in time.**

Some people may wonder what at what I am able to see in a block. I am also amazed at the number of images I see that correspond to this life or a former one.

Inner images are especially important for me in remote constellations. I lay a block down for a certain theme and I see an entire film play before me. Even here I test my images before assuming that they are correct.

Intuition can be learned.

The more I've learned to trust my inner images, the more they have shown me. In my training groups, I not only teach a systemic concept, but also place great value on supporting each individual's intuition. Intuitive perception is an indispensable tool in my field of work!

A promise leads us to hope,

keeping it to dread.

François de La Rochefoucauld, Reflections

NEW RESOLUTION STATEMENTS

For release from promises, oaths, vows and contracts of the soul from present and previous lives

An additional new method of integrative family constellation is the release from promises, oaths, vows and contracts of the soul from this and previous lives. I have compiled a list of new resolution statements for release from various entanglements. Since the necessary resolution statements can be formulated many ways, I have only listed those that figure frequently in my experience in this summary. If one of the resolution statements appeals to you, then you can use it to resolve your own entanglements by speaking it aloud or mentally reciting it to the respective person or institution.

PROMISES

Releasing yourself from promises
Assuming belief systems and feelings from our ancestors or from previous lives is often associated with a promise. In this case, I cannot let go of what I have assumed without releasing myself from a promise. We unconsciously carry a number of promises within us that we have given to our parents, grandparents, siblings, partners and others from this and previous lives.

Examples of promises in a partnership:
"I promise to only love you and remain forever faithful to you."
"I promise to always feel responsible for you."
"I promise that I will never leave you."
"I promise to conceive children only with you."

Resolution statements to release yourself from promises in a partnership:
"I release myself from the promise to love only you and remain forever faithful to you and free both you and myself for other partners." "I release myself from the promise to feel always responsible for you and now return your responsibility, power and dignity to you so that you can master your own life." "I release myself from the promise never to leave you and free you and myself from our relationship." "I release myself from the promise only to conceive children with you and now grant myself the liberty of conceiving children with another partner."

Examples of children's promises to their parents:
"I promise always to feel responsible for the failure or success of your relationship"

"In return for the opportunity to be born into this life, I promise always to place your needs above my own."

"I promise that my love and career will not succeed because yours did not succeed."

"I promise that I will never leave you, mom/dad."

Resolution statements to release yourself from children's promises to their parents:

"I release myself from the promise to feel always responsible for the failure or success of your relationship and return the responsibility to you."

"I release myself from the promise only to feel welcome with you if I place your needs above my own. Please be happy for me as I now fully focus on my needs and leave responsibility for your needs with you."

"I release myself from the promise not to allow myself success in my love and professional life because yours did not succeed. Please be happy for me as I am allowed to succeed in love and my job.
I thank you."

"Dear mom/dad, I release myself from the promise never to leave you and now free myself for my own life."

For a practical example, see Case 13: "Careful during sex!" – fear of accepting the masculine.

In many other cases it becomes clear that releasing yourself from promises is an important aspect of a good solution.

My lips did give the oath,

but not my heart.

Euripides, Hippolytus

OATHS AND VOWS

Dissolving oaths and vows
Oaths and vows are primarily found in our previous lives. These can be oaths of revenge as well as love. Oaths are often made in the context of religious institutions. Time and again I see that my clients still carry vows of chastity from a previous life as a priest, monk or nun which can pose hindrances to their current sex-lives. Even religious vows of marriage must be consciously dissolved in order to completely free oneself from a relationship and be free for a new partnership.

Examples of oaths and vows
"I pledge before God to remain your spouse so long as we both shall live."
"I swear always to be loyal and serve you."
"I swear before God always to protect you."
"I vow to take revenge on you."

Resolution statements for release from oaths and vows:
"I hereby break my pledge to remain your spouse as long as we both shall live and release us both from it."
"I hereby break my oath always to be loyal and serve you, and release myself for my own life. I now leave responsibility for your lives with you. I now reclaim all of the power, strength and dignity which I relinquished to you. We are now equals."
"I hereby break my oath always to protect you and now release myself from it. I now return the responsibility for your protection to you."
"I hereby break my vow to take revenge against you and now reconcile with you."

Vows to religious institutions
These often stem from previous lives as nuns or priests:
"I vow only to love God." - a divested vow of chastity

Resolution statements for release from religious vows:
"I hereby break my vow to only love God and now release myself for love to all people."
"I hereby release myself from my vows of chastity, to renounce the body, sexual desire and worldly things and allow myself to fully fulfill my human needs again."
For practical examples, see Case 9: "I can't orgasm" – a vow of chastity, Case 17 Physical pain as an offset for guilt and Case 24: "Things can't go well for me" – blocked joy for life.

*Those who cannot exist without one other
are better off parting ways.*

Friedrich Schiller, The Maid of Orleans

CONTRACTS OF THE SOUL

Dissolving contracts of the soul
Before we are physically incarnated into this life on earth, we conclude various contracts of the soul. For this journey, we choose the people with whom we can successfully pass the learning experiences we need. In this sense, we determine the people we encounter as parents, children and partners, how long these relationships should last and what roles should be played (i.e. victim-perpetrator, the charitable benefactor or the envious miser, the jealous or resentful type, etc.). In our subconscious, we have an approximate plan of what and who to expect in this life, how long these relationships should last, whether learning experiences should serve for the short term or for an entire lifetime. We are internally oriented to one another and so do not meet each other coincidentally, rather, because of a long-planned agreement to fulfill our commitments to the best of our abilities. However, these are by no means unchangeable! Since we are equipped with a free will, we have the option to change or prematurely terminate a contract at any time. Most contracts will be maintained with regards to the respective learning experience, but it may also happen that people and circumstances develop differently than originally planned.

Contracts of the soul on a partnership level
These agreements are not just made within the framework of church weddings, but rather prior to incarnation. I only experience the dissolution of contracts of the soul if one partner begins to block the other's development. These separations are not done frivolously. Most people unconsciously sense that they are bound to their partner by a strong bond that is not easily broken. Many things are tried in order to save the relationship until sooner or later one of the partners finally throws in the towel. However, going through separation and even divorce does not automatically dissolve the concluded contract of the soul. Even months or years after the separation, people may still feel that they are not yet free from their ex-partner. Only by consciously dissolving the old contract of the soul is one truly free for a new relationship.

Examples of lifelong contracts of the soul between partners
Jenny, to her ex-husband Donald:
"I hereby release myself from our contract of the soul to remain together with you as your lifelong partner and now free both you and myself from it. This old agreement is no longer viable for me because I can no longer develop together with you."
For more information see Case 15: Doubts about fatherhood – an insecure identity.

When contracts of the soul cannot be fulfilled
Even with the best intentions, originally agreed contracts of the soul cannot always be maintained. If a contract cannot be fulfilled, then it must be dissolved so that both parties can release each other from guilt and responsibility.

Examples of contracts of the soul that cannot be fulfilled
Marla has been separated from her ex-partner, Gary, for more than a year. She has gotten over him, but simultaneously feels that she can't fully open herself to her new partner, Ron. The results of my testing show that she is not yet free from Gary. While looking over their mutual contract of the soul, I discover that she has agreed to lead him to his spirituality in this life. Since Gary continuously blocked Marla's spiritual interest over their three-year relationship, she was unable to fulfill this contract. She unconsciously feels guilty towards him and doesn't allow herself to enter into a new relationship. We dissolve this contract with the following phrases:

Dissolving the contract of the soul
Marla to Gary:
"Dear Gary, I now release myself from our contract of the soul to lead you to your spirituality. I did the best I could. I now leave responsibility for your spiritual development with you." Marla is relieved and test results show that she no longer has feelings of guilt towards him; she is now free for her new relationship

Example of a contract of the soul that cannot be fulfilled
Christina had a three-year relationship with Leon. He was the first person with whom she could imagine having a family and Leon also had plans for the future with her. However, since faithfulness wasn't his strong suit, Christina ended the relationship.
Today, 4½ years later, she wants to have a baby with her current partner, Randy. They just can't seem to conceive and she wants to assess this hindrance with me. In the individual constellation a contract of the soul with Leon appears, in which both have agreed to a lifelong partnership and to having a child together. Christina is internally still bound to this contract.

Dissolving the contract of the soul
Christina to Leon:
"Dear Leon, I now release myself from our contract to have a child together with you and to remain with you in a lifelong relationship. I now free both you and myself from it."

Christina is now confident that she can conceive a baby with Randy.

ADDITIONAL HELPFUL RESOLUTION STATEMENTS

Examples for the dissolution of assumed doctrines from institutions
"I now relinquish all of the negative doctrines that I have assumed from the institution ____ (specify), that sexuality, desire and my body are something dirty for which I must be ashamed."
"I release myself from the doctrine whereby the only purpose of sexuality is to conceive children."
"I now surrender myself to physical desire and the enjoyment of worldly pleasures once again. These are all granted by God and meant for my happiness."

Examples of dissolving assumed concepts of suffering
"I release myself from the concept that life is the fall of mankind, for which I must feel guilt. I see my life as a self-determined learning process in the duality of "good and evil" and assume responsibility for this decision. Experiencing both leads me to completeness and back to divine unity."

Resolution statements to regain relinquished power and strength
"I now reclaim all of the power and strength that I have relinquished to the institution of ____ (specify)."
"I release myself from the commandments and prohibitions of this institution and once again trust my own internal divine guidance."
"I have a direct relationship with God."
From the time of the Inquisition, women in particular are still bound to coerced promises that they would never again reveal the truth and instead abdicate their own inner wisdom and healing powers.

Resolution statements to regain dissociated feminine facets
"I now fully and completely reclaim all of the feminine power, strength and dignity as a woman, which I relinquished to the institution of ____ (specify)."
"I now release myself from the following promises I have imposed on myself:"

– "I will never see again (pertaining to physical seeing and clairvoyance)."
– "I will never feel again (physical, emotional and extrasensory perception)."
– "I will never again speak my truth (usually blocked throat chakra)."
– "I am not worthy of being a priestess."

Positive reformulations to integrate dissociated feminine facets
– "I once again allow myself to see fully and completely and open my third eye to my clairvoyance to the degree that it is beneficial for me."
– "I allow myself to feel again. I am now secure in my body and allow myself to perceive everything that my souls wishes to reveal to me, whether others understand it or not."

– "I allow myself once again to express my inner truth fully and completely."
– "I release myself from the assumed concept that God is masculine."
– "I recognize the masculine and feminine power in God and allow the divine feminine power to manifest itself in me again."
– "I allow myself to integrate my priestess once again. As a woman, I am worthy of being a divine channel and bearer of divine dignity."

Resolution statements to dissolve black magic bonds

Many people have had incarnations as teachers or students of black magic. Often, old bonds in our current lives remain from the promises made in that time.

– "I release myself from all promises and pacts to serve the power of black magic."
– "I release myself from the teacher-pupil relationship and reclaim all of the power and strength that I relinquished to my teacher(s). I am my own master."
– "I also release myself from my promise to my teacher(s) to relinquish energy."
– "I am grateful for everything I was able to learn from my teachers and now leave it be."
– "As a former teacher of black magic, I now release all pupils who are still energetically bound to me. You are your own masters and no longer need to relinquish energy to me."

The following phrases have been proven to fully and completely restore one's own creative power and strength without fear of misusing them once more:

– "I now bind my power and strength to my heart and place it into the service of the whole. I now serve love and the light."

*Who can deny that our lives would be easier
if we were not accompanied by an unbroken chain of curses of the
most select caliber?
However, one may never stoop to those of mean grades.*

Heimito von Doderer, Repertorium

CURSES

Dissipating curses:
Curses spoken out of intense resentment, sorrow or jealousy can remain in effect for generations. However, curses only work if the person(s) affected carries a feeling of guilt; otherwise a curse has no power over him.

Examples of spoken curses:
"You shall always be wanderers and never find a home again!" "You will never have children!"

Resolution statements to dissipate such curses:
"I now free you from my curse that you shall never find a home and bless the ground beneath your feet. You may now enter your home again!'
"I now break the curse I placed on you that you would never have children. I now bless your children's birth."

Resolution for those who have been cursed:
For those who believe they have been cursed, it is advisable to resolve these individually in the constellation. In order to do so, the associated feeling of guilt must be recognized and released.

There are people who so ardently and resolutely desire something that, for fear of falling short, they never forget to do that which will hinder their success.

Jean de La Bruyere, The Characters

INABILITY TO HAVE CHILDREN

Causes from this and previous lives

Couples keep coming to me to see why they have been unable to fulfill their long-standing desire to have children. I know this problem very well from my own experience. It doesn't only affect those who give birth later in life, but also many younger couples around 30 years of age. As a foundation, I always constellate the ancestral families of both partners. I very often find causal entanglements with ancestors that affect the conception of children.

Possible causes from the ancestral system for an inability to have children

- Entanglements with the deceased impair the strength and grounding of one's own good place in life. Unconscious feelings of guilt towards the deceased block the live-giving principle in us.
- If an ancestor died during childbirth, assumed feelings of sorrow, fear of death and fear of loss can block one's openness to procreation and subsequent birth.
- Infertile ancestors pass on their fates to those who are born later. Internally, one doesn't allow oneself to be fertile.
- Contempt for men reduces one's ability for procreation
- Mothers and their children were abandoned by their husbands
- Old feelings of guilt towards aborted children inhibit one's ability to afford a desired child a place in one's life "If you weren't allowed to come, then your siblings can't either."
- Being a wife and mother was not held in high esteem – one can't appreciate it oneself.
- One cannot accept oneself as a wife and mother due to burdensome fates such as humiliation or abuse.
- One sacrifices one's own happiness in life for the benefit of a handicapped or disadvantaged sibling.
- You can't combine motherhood and a career – motherhood is sacrificed in order to maintain a career.
- Assumed doctrines from ancestors inhibit pregnancy: fear of physical change, fear of being unable to experience sexuality during pregnancy, fear of pain during birth, etc.

These straining dynamics from our ancestral family can be complex. When a healing resolution has been developed, then the couple receives a blessing for their fertility from their ancestors. From my personal experience, see "Dear great-grandmother, I honor the loss of your four children" - Unfulfilled wish for children.

Desire for children and former lives
I very often see that it is not only family dynamics that can undermine having children, but also images and feelings from previous lives. Memories we've stored about our mothers and fathers from previous lives unconsciously affect our attitude towards having children. Traumatic experiences that we have not yet dealt with can create such a strong hindrance that even our best efforts to conceive a child can fail.

Possible causes from previous lives for an inability to have children
– Traumatic experiences related to pregnancy and birth: you or your child died during childbirth; the child was taken away after birth.
– The experience of being left alone as a wife with child: the partner died, for example in war, or abandoned you.
– Children were often aborted or given up and one feels guilt towards previous children for keeping children today.
– At the time of witch burnings, many pregnant women were burned; such traumatic experiences can cause great fears with regard to pregnancy.

There are various causes stemming from previous lives that can affect procreation and pregnancy. I have listed just a few that frequently appear in my work.

Possible causes for inability to have children on a physical level
Not everything can be solved on the emotional level, but there is a psychological issue behind every physical cause. There's a reason why, for example, a man's sperm and the mucous membrane of a woman's uterus are incompatible. That doesn't mean it can't be changed. Just as with diseases, it is worth looking beyond the physical symptoms.

Frequent questions regarding physical symptoms and the inability to have children
Why can't a woman allow her partner's sperm to enter?
Why aren't her hormone levels right? (See Case 28: Hormone deficiency – feelings of guilt from a previous life)
Why are certain essences required for pregnancy absorbed by the cell? (See Case 29: Folic acid deficiency – forbidden love as a nun)
What's behind a man's languid sperm quality?
Why can't a woman keep the fertilized egg? (See Case 27: "I'm responsible for your death" – a previous life as a babysitter).

These and many other questions can be illuminated through constellation and can very often lead to a solution.
I want to emphasize here that a constellation of physical impediments in the inability to have children is no substitute for a medical diagnosis and treatment. Rather, it is a valuable complement and support in healing.

A great man is he,

who retains the heart of a child.

James Legge, Holy Scripts of China

THE INNER CHILD IN US

As an extension of classical family constellation, integrative family constellation also comprises work with the "inner child."

What is the inner child?
The inner child in us has to do with the spontaneous, natural child who we all once were. It corresponds to the innermost core of our being. For example, it is expressed by laughing, being creative, spontaneity and amazement. Our childhood is hallmarked by our upbringing and other social influences at school, church, etc.
If we experienced too many limitations, punishments or injuries, an injured and/or modified inner child can develop from a free inner child. As an adult, we are conditioned by these influences and they determine our lives to a great extent. We repeat many familiar patterns from our childhood within our relationships, our careers and our own families.

What does work with the inner child entail?
Working with the inner child deals with healing negative childhood experiences and beliefs that negatively affect our current life. Those who experienced rejection in their childhoods and could not do right by others will later have nothing more to do with their inner child, since it is apparently not worthy of love. This leads to an extremely severe parent-self-facet in us, which perpetuates the parental negative judgment. Instead of remaining in the denouncement and victim position, we focus on assuming self-responsibility for healing these wounds. Important aspects here are developing self-love and self-acceptance instead of remaining dependent on the love of parents, partners or others. Those who wish to lead and determine their own lives must dissolve this dependence - emotional dependence in particular - on their parents. If we do not complete this step, then we remain unaltered. "I will only be loved and recognized by my parents and partner if I do this or that." If I am dependent on this love and recognition because I cannot provide it myself, then I am unable to lead my own life according to my wishes (see Case 8).

We must become children if we wish to achieve the best.

Philipp Otto Runge, Posthumous publications

Individual work with the inner child
For severe childhood injuries, I recommend that my clients purchase an inner child doll. I've personally had very good experiences with this. The doll can make

the inner child tangible. You can hold the doll in your arms and affectionately speak to it. By placing it in a conspicuous spot in your home, you can be reminded daily to perceive your inner needs. Those who have established good contact with their inner child doll can recognize at a glance how the inner child is doing and what it needs. Those who want to intensively work on the healing of their inner child can take to heart the book Das Kind in uns (The Child in Us), by John Bradshaw. It contains many exercises that allow us to love our inner child once again.

Constellating the inner child
Two additional inner facets are usually incorporated into the constellation of the personality aspect of the inner child ego. **The adult ego** = today's adult in us. **The parent ego** = influences we've adopted from our parents. In these facets, one can easily recognize which personality facet dominates our lives and how the different facets correspond to each other. Such constellations show that many people are separated from their inner child ego. They often have little or no relationship with it. The reason for this is that many of us were deprived of our childhoods. Even as very young children, we had to assume too much responsibility. Too few of our own childhood needs were perceived and fulfilled by our parents, and we forgot their importance. As a substitute, many children feel responsible for the needs of their parents while neglecting their own needs.

Those children who were not well cared for physically and emotionally have difficulties as adults in recognizing and satisfying their own needs.

In the constellation, negative beliefs about ourselves that we adopted from our parents or other influential figures are relinquished. Some beliefs stemming from hurtful or lacking childhood situations can thereby be resolved through conscious recognition.

Examples of negative beliefs
"You're not good enough – you should be perfect!" (from adopted demands for perfection)
"You're to dumb to accomplish anything!" (projected belittlement)
"I am not worthy of being loved." (from emotional neglect)
"We married only because of you." (adopted projection of guilt)
"I will only be loved if I
...ignore my own needs."
...always feel responsible and guilty for everything."
...am an exemplary child."
...repress my own negative feelings."
...if I do well enough."
...etc.

Instead of negative beliefs, we can instill positive assessments of ourselves. Within the constellation, you have the possibility to embrace your inner child and tell it how important and valuable it is for you! You can tell your inner child everything that it has always longed for.

Examples for instilling positive beliefs
"I am perfectly fine as I am."
"I love myself as I am."
"I am allowed to make mistakes."
"I have everything I need to realize my goals in life."
"I am worthy of love just as I am."

> **We all long for unconditional love, to simply be accepted as we are. The first step to doing this is to affectionately accept ourselves and to be the parents that we would have hoped for.**

The inner child and previous lives
Our current life is the most important factor that influences our self-value and the ability to accept ourselves. The fact that we perhaps experienced a not-so-rosy childhood in this life may stem from karmic feelings of guilt from previous lives. Very often I see that people who suffered an oppressive childhood were very powerful rulers in previous lives who misused their power. I today's life, they want to play the role of the oppressed and thereby strike a balance. In the same way, people who had very self-centered, egocentric learning experiences in previous lives concentrate on the needs of others and often work in helping, caring professions in this life to find balance again. Once the learning process has reached the opposite extreme, the pendulum of life swings back in the other direction. It can be about myself and others; I can control and you can, too (see Case 10: Being free for your own family – assuming a father's power and strength).

CASE STUDIES FROM MY PRACTICE

General

Thanks to my clients, I am able to provide concrete cases from my own experience. I have chosen those topics that frequently appear and affect many of us. These cases are presented anonymously with the consent of my clients, which is why I have altered all of the names and ages. To precisely depict the procedure of my integrative family constellation, I have presented Case 1 in its entirety. Since this thorough narration is too comprehensive for all cases, I have concisely summarized the important steps and results of my work in all subsequent cases.

A = Advisor
C = Client

Case 1

"I'm afraid of my clients" – Balancing guilt with atonement

Individual constellation
Glenda S., 44 years old, self-employed, divorced, 2 children from her first marriage

Glenda S. comes to my home for an individual constellation. She appears to be seeking help as she explains her problem to me:

C: "I'm in a state of fear. On my way to work, I prefer to creep past the people I see with averted eyes. I'm embarrassed when someone speaks to me; I also don't want to have to serve customers in my business. It's a very unpleasant situation for me, because I have to make sales and at the same time I hope that no customers enter my office. This can't go on like this – I have to find a solution!"
A: "How long have you had these fears?"
C: "For about two months."
A: "Was there perhaps an event that could have triggered this behavior?"
C: "Not directly, but as you know I've been struggling with the idea of selling my business for quite some time. It's no longer financially feasible for me, even though I invest almost all of my time in my career."
A: "Have you experienced these kinds of fears before?"
C: "No, not like this. This is the first time."
A: "Ms. S., is it okay for you if I slip into your role in order to form an impression of your situation?"

Individual constellation with a pillow

C: "Yes. Should I choose a pillow for myself? Do I need anything else?"

A: "Yes, please choose a pillow for yourself and one for that which you are afraid of."

Note: C chooses two pillows and lays these diagonal to one another - I assume her role.

A: I describe my perceptions to my client:
"I see myself standing with a bowed head in a small, basement-like recess. It's dark and I only have a couple of thin slots that connect me to the outside world. Outside I see people standing; they are staring and pointing at me. I feel ashamed."

C: "Yes, that's how I feel – that pretty much describes it exactly!"

A: I look to the other pillow (that which I'm afraid of):
"The pillow appears very bright; I see people standing in the light who are highly successful and live their lives with strength and happiness. It appears as through everyone may stand in the light except for me." I feel sorrow welling up inside me.

C: "Yes, I'm familiar with this feeling." The client appears affected and begins to cry.

A: "Together with me, please lay down another pillow to represent the cause of your feelings of being excluded."

C lays down a light yellow pillow in front of me.

A: I describe my image to her: "I see myself as a king in a beautiful palace." (It may have been one of my client's previous lives.) I now sit on the pillow in order to glean more information. My body automatically assumes the posture of a king. "I perceive that he is focused on decorating his palace with beautiful paintings. He appears to be primarily fixated on himself and the aesthetic objects around him."

C: "You know, that reminds me of my father. He was that kind of man. He built us a giant house with all of the amenities. He had a certain penchant for megalomania."

A: "That may be, but I stand for you, not for your father. At that time, you may also have been inclined to grandeur and luxury."

C: Laughs and says, "Yes, my first husband also had a nice, big house that we lived in, but I lost it due to the divorce. We also lost the house that my father built for us due to bankruptcy."

A: "Please give me another pillow so that I can see what happened then."

Note: C lays down a dark pillow.

A: "When I look at it I see the people; symbolically they seem fettered and bleeding. Their king seems to deprive them of their land and thereby their livelihood." I am still sitting on the king's pillow and also sense that he considers the people riffraff and cares little for them. He is too fixated on himself."

Note: I ask Ms. S to sit on the pillow representing the people and to slip into this image.

C: "I know this feeling well; I'm fighting to survive, a very futile fight!"

A: "It appears to me like a guilt/atonement balance, in which you have chosen the role of the bleeding people in this life. What do you think about everything that has appeared up to now?"
C: "Yes, I've been so ashamed of myself recently. I'm afraid that the people are pointing at me. Everything appears to make sense, but how can I overcome this?"

Resolving the previous life
A: "I recommend that you take the inner role of the king who you previously were, bow before your people and ask for forgiveness for ruling without compassion." Together we ask that the power of Christ support us so that light, love and forgiveness can flow into her previous life and touch the people who suffered at that time. Ms. S bows before the pillow representing the people and feels a burden on her shoulders. A: "I ask that you let this burden go and forgive yourself for your behavior at that time."
C: "Everything is becoming lighter and easier around me."
A: "I also sense that the people are now very peaceful. Now, please turn to the king who you once were and take the pillow in your arms, so that you can also reintegrate his strong and powerful personality. Now, however, you will rule for the people (I give Ms. S the pillow representing the people) and use your power with love and compassion. This way, you will not only think of yourself, but of others."
C: "That feels good, very harmonious. You know, I have recently joined an organization for which I work part time selling products and earning extra money. However, a part of the profit automatically goes to a charity - like cancer societies, aid for children in Africa, etc."
A: "That sounds like a wonderful opportunity to integrate both facets!"
C: "I think so, too. I now understand my motivation and the context that led me to this organization much better."
A: "How do you feel now? Do you still feel afraid? How do you feel about the looks of the people standing in the light?" (I point at the pillow).

Effect of the resolution steps
C: "I feel strong again; the shame is gone. Now I can stand in the light with the others."
A: "How do you feel about the thought of approaching others to sell them something?"
C: "It doesn't stress me anymore. I can work from within again and negotiate. How did that suddenly become so much easier?"
A: "It may be the strength and power that you've regained from the king, which allows you to be creative and to negotiate again. How do you perceive yourself?"
C: "I stand taller, I feel more self-value, more dignity in myself."
A: "When I place your business in front of you, how do you perceive it?" Note: I place a pillow representing the business in front of my client.

C: "It seems that I look beyond it: for a long time it hasn't made sense for me to go there and withhold my energy. Right now, I perceive myself more with the need to be happy and to accentuate my femininity. I haven't really done that for a long time. I think I'll soon find a solution for the business - perhaps a buyer. I have an appointment concerning this in two weeks."
A: "Yes, I also think that ending this old guilt/atonement routine will have positive effects for your business. Please let me know how things develop."
C: "Yes, I'll definitely do that. Right now I feel very good and I hope that I can keep this feeling for the long run."
A: "I'm certain you will. You've done everything you need to ensure that."

Feedback two weeks later
Glenda S. calls me to let me know that she has fully resolved her business fears. Sales have become easier for her again. She can approach clients without feeling guilty.

CASE 2

"Dear twin brother, I miss you!" – Candace's growth on her left kidney

Individual constellation
Candace H., 26 years old, single, no children

Candace comes to me and seems extremely worn out. She tells me about a growth on her left kidney. She was advised to have an operation. She wanted to find out the psychological causes of the growth. She suspects that there is a correlation with the cramped living quarters in her boyfriend's house. She and her boyfriend share a house with his parents and sister.

Pillow placement:
After we've discussed the dynamics of her ancestral family as a basis, I ask her to choose and lay down one pillow for herself, her partner, the growth and the common living situation respectively. She places a pleasant-looking pillow with blue roses for the growth to her right, the pillow representing her boyfriend is set slightly away from her and the pillow for the living situation is placed opposite.

Perception:
Since the client has trouble identifying the latent dynamics in her situation, I offer to act her role for her.

A in Candace's stead: "I sense that someone is missing and recognize that the pillow representing the growth stands for my unborn twin brother from multiple fertilization (see Ch. ...). I am very happy to be aware of him; I'm not interested in anything else at present." I now ask Candace to take her place herself. In the meanwhile, I do kinesiologic testing to see if my perception of the twin brother is correct. The result is a clear yes with the arm length test (see Ch. ...) .....).

Candace H. in her seat: Appears deeply moved and says, "I've always felt like I've lacked someone, that I've been so alone in this world." Since twins are very intensely connected with each other, I recommend that Candace do a group constellation so that she can easily perceive her twin brother as a human being. Candace agrees to this and seems more at ease, since she no longer sees the growth as a threat, but rather as something familiar to her.

Continuation during an open evening group
This time, I ask Candace only to constellate herself and her unborn twin brother. Once again, she places both pillows very close to one another, her brother on her right side (partner side).

Representative for Candace: She appears simultaneously happy and sad as she hugs her twin brother with the words, "I've missed you so much – I finally have you again!"

Representative for twin brother: Candace observes the scene and cries. I let her take her place in order to feel the nearness to her brother. Letting go of her twin brother is possible only after she's allowed this inner nearness and can accept him. It takes a while until both of them can release themselves from this inner hug.

Resolution statement:
Candace to her twin brother: "Dear brother, I am only complete with you; you are a part of me. I now grant you a good place in my heart – I'll never lose you again. Our connection will continue even after your death. I will now continue with my life. Please smile kindly on me, so that I can remain at peace. Please be my protector and bless me for my life."

Twin brother to Candace: "I bless you from my world and will always be there for you when you need me." Additionally, I now ask Candace's twin brother to speak the following resolution statement to his sister: "I now release you for your life and for the men in your life." When releasing her for the men in her life, he stumbles somewhat. This is a sign that theirs was not only a brother-sister relationship, but also previously a partner relationship.

Resolution statement to resolve a previous life as a partner
Candace to her twin brother: "I now release all of the old karmic entanglements between us and grant both you and myself freedom from all promises and contracts that bound us as partners."

Twin brother: Hesitates a little, but is then also ready to release old partner ties with the assurance that they will see each other once again after Candace's death. Until then, she should be free. Candace is also very slow to release her brother. She will need additional time to process the release from him.

Feedback 1 year later
Candace's life has changed considerably since our last session. She tells me that she separated from her boyfriend two months prior and has now moved to another city. She's doing well with the changes. Candace: "It was urgently necessary!" The growth on her left kidney was surgically removed six months prior. The kidney is symbolic of partnership - old relationship structures in Candace's life have been resolved through the separation from her partner and the operation (release from her twin brother). A new phase has begun in Candace's life.

CASE 3

Finding your own path in life – freedom from slavery and external control

Remote constellation

Gabriele S. is 44 years old, married and the mother of 2 children

Gabriele has been to one-on-one therapy in my office, since she wants to physically separate herself from her husband. He is very aggressive towards her and the children. She was forced on several occasions to seek refuge at a women's shelter. She no longer wants this for herself and her children. Her son already suffers from hearing problems, since he tries to block out his parent's fighting. Meanwhile, she has found an apartment for herself and the children. Her husband is unaware of this. Gabriele: "I'm really afraid to tell him that I'm leaving with the children. He will certainly be very angry and try to stop me." She asks me to determine the best time to move into the new apartment in a remote constellation.

Remote constellation
In the remote constellation, I take one pillow for Gabriele, one for her husband and one for the new apartment, which will be available at the beginning of next month.

Perceiving Gabriele: I feel that I lack the courage to take that first step and move into the apartment, although I already find myself ready to abandon ship. I'm afraid of my husband - that he'll be angry and won't let me go.
Perceiving the husband: I feel that he perceives me as his property, that he can do what he wants with me. He doesn't want to let me go.

I place an additional pillow between the two in order to determine where Gabriele's fear and impulse towards servitude originate, which stop her from deciding her own life.

Gabriele as a slave in a previous life

Perceiving the new location: I see Gabriele as a black African slave in a previous life. Her head is lowered; her will is completely broken. She has relinquished her independence and responsibility for her life to her master at the time (who is her current husband). She serves him with her labor in return for his provision of food. She doesn't have any other privileges.

Effects on her current life

Gabriele cannot yet take back her freedom. She still carries these old feeling of belonging to someone else, whom she must obey. She does not have the authority to make decisions about her own life.

Resolution statements for the resolution of her previous life as a slave

Gabriele to her husband: "I now take back all of the power, dignity, freedom and responsibility that I relinquished to you earlier. I am now ready to accept responsibility for myself. You are now free of your responsibility for me. I am no longer your servant and slave; I am not your property. I hereby release all entanglements and promises from that life. I can go my own way at any time. I belong only to myself and only I have authority over my life. I am now free of every type of enslavement. I allow myself to live in complete freedom!"

Debriefing

Directly after the remote constellation, I tell Gabriele that now is the time to begin the process of liberating herself from the old victim and slave roles and to regain responsibility for her own life. As soon as she is able to take care of herself and her own life, then she will manage the move to her new apartment without any trouble. I recommend an individual session in order to support her in this effort. Furthermore, I also give her the resolution statements above to help her on her way. She should mentally speak and internalize the phrases 3 times per week.

Feedback 2 months later

Gabriele has moved into the first apartment of her own. She says, "Until my husband can treat me with more kindness, I will not go back to him." The children live with her for the time being.

CASE 4

"You abandoned me" - the path to your own life energy

Remote constellation
Helen K. is 56 years old, widowed and the mother of one son.

In individual sessions with me, Helen has set up constellations of her ancestral family as well as her present family. Her father has recently been in the hospital because of a heart attack. She takes care of him regularly. Since her retirement income is very limited, he has offered to support her financially. However, his verbal capacity is limited because of the heart attack, and he therefore cannot help her. For about two weeks, Helen has suffered from what she describes as a "spiritual pain." Helen: "I am sad and have a sense of failure." Since she is from another state, she asks me to have a closer look at the psychological causes of her pain via remote constellation.

Remote constellation:
I place pillows representing Helen, her spiritual pain and her father.
Perception with Helen: her spiritual pain and her father appear to be joined as one unit. At the same time, I feel an energy pulling me back. I turn around and sense a man who is pulling at me. My first impulse in the representative role is towards Helen's first husband, who committed suicide. I received the same result when verifying this.
Note: In Helen's present constellation, I can remember that it was very difficult for her to forgive her husband. He committed suicide many years ago and left her and her son alone. She had to try very hard not to make negative remarks about him in front of her son.
I place a pillow for her deceased husband as well.
Perception with Helen: I perceive that I am still angry with him and that I haven't forgiven him yet. I have therefore bound him to me and he cannot go on in peace.
I place another pillow to represent what is necessary in order to forgive him.
Perception with Helen: I recognize images of a previous life with him.

Helen has abandoned her husband in a previous life

Perception with Helen: He was also my partner at that time. He was violent and I was very afraid of him. When he committed theft and had to go to jail, a very influential male friend of mine helped me ensure that he wouldn't be released quickly. Although I could have used my influential friend to help him, I abandoned him. I suddenly feel guilty! It appears that this friend is my current father.
Consequences on Helen's current life
Just as Helen abandoned her husband back then, he abandoned her and their son

with his premature death in this life. In this life, she was forced to experience the opposite role.

Release from the previous life
Perception with Helen: I am now ready to allow healing and forgiveness to flow into this old life and ask forgiveness from my dead husband for what I did to him. I now turn back to my father and the spiritual pain connected with him. Between myself and my father I place a pillow representing what is necessary in order to recognize the cause of this pain and heal it.

In this pillow, I see abysms from numerous lives that I've lived with my father. One of them is the life with my dead husband, where together we abandoned him. I feel that now is the time to accept responsibility for my previous life and to liberate myself from the role of the poor victim.

My father has also left me in a lurch financially in this life. Only now can I recognize the gift from both men to me. I understand that today's task is to find my own strength and especially to find personal independence. All at once, the spiritual pain subsides. I no longer have the feeling of being a downtrodden victim of destiny who is not worthy of receiving gifts and support. I now feel stronger!

Debriefing:
I subsequently inform Helen of my perception that the key is to privately release both men, since in the meanwhile she has learned to manage well on her own. Helen: "My husband's suicide placed large demands on me and showed me all that I could do as a single mother."
Helen can relate to the images I saw and I give her the following resolution statements:

Resolution statements for resolving previous and current lives
Helen to her deceased husband: "I forgive you for leaving so soon. Please forgive me as well for leaving you alone to sit in jail in our previous life. I did not remain at your side; I was very afraid of you and couldn't act otherwise. I now accept my part of the responsibility for everything between us and I leave your part of the responsibility with you. I now accept responsibility for my life and you are free from it. I have also managed without you; it has made me strong."

I now ask Helen to let healing and forgiveness flow from her heart into this life.

Feedback 11 months later
Helen: "My father passed away last Christmas. I spent many hours with him in the nursing home. We laughed and cried together and became very close! You

really helped me. I also went through trauma therapy, which helped to release a lot of old pain. I am no longer burdened by my ex-husband – all of that is now far removed from me."

CASE 5

A lack of income – competition with my father in a previous life

Remote constellation
Markus L. is 32 years old, married and has 2 children

Markus works in the field of physical energy therapy. He calls me and complains about too few clients and a lack of income. He asks me to perform a remote constellation in order to determine the causes and to resolve them with him.

Remote constellation with blocks
I place the following people in the picture: Markus, his income and the hindrance to it. Regarding the income, I recognize that it is willing to flow to him, but that his low self-esteem won't allow it. With kinesiologic testing, I see his mother as the hindrance to his self-value.

Resolution statement for Markus:
Markus to his mother: "Dear mother, I take your feeling of not being good enough as a wife and return it to you with love. Please look kindly upon me when I now feel worthy as a husband. I thank you!"
With regard to his mother, I see another karmic partnership entanglement from a previous life. Since it doesn't appear important to explore this life more closely, we dissolve this connection with the following statements:

Resolution statements to resolve previous and current lives
Markus to his mother: "Dear mother, I hereby resolve all karmic partnership entanglements between us and all promises to love only you forever. I now release both you and me from them. I am no longer your partner; I am your son and now take you into my heart as my mother. Father is the right partner for you, not me – I am your child."
Markus to his present father: "Dear father, you are mother's partner, not me. You give and I take – you are the better partner for mother."

Consequences of his previous life on his paternal relationship and current income
The father figure stands for self realization, our orientation in life and therefore

also for our success and the income associated with it. Those who cannot accept their fathers into their hearts will probably have blockages to overcome. This true for Markus, who was unable to accept his father because of a previous life. When I do a kinesiologic test to see whether everything hindering his income has been resolved, I see yet another blockage from a previous life with his father, which has also hampered his ability to accept him into his heart.

Rivalry and jealousy with my father in a previous life
Markus and his current father were previously siblings. He was the younger brother and always had to fight for a place at his father's side, because the older brother was more loved. Markus placed the blame on his brother for his feeling of not receiving enough love from their father. He resented him and tried to belittle him in order to make himself seem bigger and stronger. He no longer wanted to be the underdog. Markus tells me later that still today he has a tendency to feel insecure around his father and to be in constant competition with him.

Learning experience for Markus
When I asked what Markus had to learn from this experience, I received the following realization: he had to learn to be disadvantaged in order to measure his worth not against external contributions, but his own capacity as a human being.

Resolution statements to resolve previous and current lives
<u>Markus to his current father</u> (who was then his brother): "Dear father, I now take all of the power, dignity and strength that I relinquished to you, because I thought that you were the better of us both. I will stop comparing myself to you and recognize my own value. You are no longer my big brother, but my father. You are fine as you are and I am fine as I am. Thank you for my life. You are the right father for me, and I am both like and unlike you. I now take you to heart as my father and you may take me as your son. Please give me your blessing and strength in being a husband and a father as well as in my professional life, even if I earn my money differently to you. I respect your profession and your values; please respect mine as well. I thank you!"

Debriefing
Markus can relate to the constellation images and will speak the resolution statements until he senses an inner feeling of resolution.

Feedback one year later
Markus: "I'm doing very well. In the meanwhile I am in a well-paying salaried position. I am very satisfied with my income. Since I no longer have to depend solely on the energy therapy, the financial pressure on me is gone and I have enough clients."

CASE 6

"My partner is unable to open up to me" – Fear of losing power

Individual constellation

Sandra N. is 34 years old, single and has no children

Sandra is coming for a debriefing of her original family constellation, which took place one month prior. Sandra: "I feel very good. Many of my self-esteem problems are gone. The bullying situation at work has gotten better. I am valued and respected more by my boss and colleagues. I'm especially happy that my mother called for the first time in 30 years and joined me for a coffee. She was very interested in the constellation work I've done with you." Sandra is very moved because she has never experienced such a good relationship with her family. The only thing that still bears heavily on her is her long-term relationship with her boyfriend, Christian. They have been living separately for four months. Sandra still loves him as before and can't seem to give him up. Sandra: "I believe that his family situation blocks him from fully opening up to me. I'd like to look at the situation with him again."

Individual constellation with pillows
Sandra places pillows to represent herself and Christian.

Perception at Sandra's spot: I feel very good. When I look at Christian's pillow, I feel what it would be like if he were completely open to me. I feel a sense of fear welling up within me. I ask Sandra to place a pillow in order to determine where this fear originates.
Perception at Sandra's spot: Now I recognize my fear of losing power and control over the relationship. A kinesiologic test shows that this fear comes from Sandra's paternal grandmother.
Sandra places both of her grandparents into the picture. At the grandmother's spot, I sense that her grandfather is the family patriarch and that her grandmother does what he feels is right. Sandra releases herself from the acquired role of her grandmother with the following statements:

Resolution statements
Sandra to her grandmother: "Dear grandma, I lovingly relinquish your belief that men should be in the leadership role and have the ultimate say in a relationship. I also give back the feeling of having little value as a woman and the inability to participate equally in marriage. Please look kindly upon me, as I am now able to feel equal as a woman in a relationship and do not relinquish my power to my partner."

At the grandmother's spot: "Dear Sandra, I am happy that you can stand next to your partner as an equal and lead your lives together." Sandra, who receives her grandmother's blessing in her own spot, feels relieved and thanks her grandmother. I go to Sandra's spot once again in order to see what has changed in the relationship with Christian. In her spot, I have a need to tell him that I cannot relinquish my power and strength to him within our relationship. During kinesiologic testing I see another blockage that relates to a previous life:

Sandra is Christian's mother in a previous life
I ask Sandra to place a pillow representing this previous life. I thereby recognize that Sandra was once Christian's mother. I see images that tell me Christian was antagonized by his father. The reason for this was that he was not his real father; Sandra had passed off her illegitimate son as his own.

Sandra places an additional pillow for the real father and resolves the systemic entanglements with the following statements:

Resolution statements for resolving previous lives
Sandra to her former partner (whom she misled with her illegitimate son): "I'm sorry for what I did. I was unable to do better."
Sandra to the real father: "You are the real father. I now give back responsibility for your son. I'm sorry that I never told you that you are his father." Sandra takes a deep breath. She feels relieved now that she can free herself from this secret.

Consequences on her current life
Sandra tells me that on an emotional level, she is affected by all of the altercations between Christian and his parents. Sandra: "He doesn't stand up for himself to them and then he vents all of his frustration on me. I'm just happy that he expresses these feelings and I absorb everything." I test to see why Sandra lets herself be the receptacle for all of his negative feelings. I recognize that she still carries feelings of guilt from her former role as his mother, because she stood by helplessly as her former husband hit and antagonized him. To counteract this guilt, she now accepts his aggression.

Resolution statements
Sandra to Christian: "I'm sorry that I didn't spare you the physical and psychological abuse as my son at that time. I now expect you to take the experience that you had in choosing to be my child and I accept only my part of the responsibility. Today I am no longer your mother! I now return your strength and dignity as a man as well as your responsibility for your life." In perceiving the roles, I see that Christian can now grow and that Sandra now feels equal next to him. She has released herself from her role as a mother and from all of the guilt and sense that she always had to make something up to him.

Feedback 8 months later
Sandra: "After our constellation I felt equal as a woman towards Christian; the motherly feelings are gone. My self-confidence as a woman has improved so much that I now have no problem separating myself from his negative feelings. I am officially no longer affected by him. Christian had said, "You're just not you any more!" I could leave him as he was and I've separated from him in the meantime. I now feel more happiness in life."

CASE 7

Guilt and atonement through rheumatic pain – Denied love for oneself

Individual constellation

Katie S. is 48 years old, widowed and without children

Katie comes to me complaining of rheumatic pains that she's been unable to heal for 15 years. She would like to see the psychological causes of her illness with an individual constellation.

Individual constellation with pillows
Katie places a pillow for herself and one directly across from her to represent her illness. During testing, I see that the rheumatism is an unborn twin sister from multiple fertilization. She's excited to hear about the twin sister.

Perception in Katie's position: "I feel stiff, as if I'm frozen solid. My breath is anxious and flat. I sense my twin sister like a burden on me; everything around me is dark. I now see images of when we were together in the womb. At the moment when my twin sister died and left me, I entered a state of panic and now have the feeling that I'm unable to move. I want to follow her so that I don't have to stay behind alone. I feel alone and unable to survive. A wave of guilt passes over me. It's as if I just can't manage life alone."

Feelings of guilt for the death of a sister in a previous life
Perception in Katie's position: "I now see an image from a previous life in which we were sisters. While we were playing, she suddenly fell into a well. It was as if I was unconscious and was unable to help her. My sister drowned in the well. I see my parents as they blame me for her death.

Resolution statements to resolve previous lives
Katie to her then-parents: "I now return the parental guilt and responsibility

that I acquired from you at that time. I was only a child. I am not to blame for my sister's death - you were the adults. I was the child."

Katie feels a great sense of relief. I ask her to take her sister to heart with the following statements:
Katie to her sister: "Dear sister, you must accept the responsibility for your destiny and your death. I leave it with you. You will always have a special place in my heart. Please look kindly upon me so that I can lead a good life."

It's difficult for Katie to let go of her sister. I sense an old promise that she's previously made to her sister.

Katie to her sister: "I now absolve myself from the promise we made to always stay together; we are now freed from it. I can manage now without you, but only with your blessing."
Katie takes her sister's pillow and hugs it tightly. Now it is easier for her to let her go. We test her rheumatism again. Its pillow is now further away from her and no longer appears so threatening. A kinesiologic test shows that another guilt-atonement issue from a previous life is at the root of her illness and needs to be resolved. Katie now places a pillow to represent what's necessary to free herself from these burdens. When perceiving at this position, I sense that she lacks self-love, especially the ability to feel love purely for herself. I recommend a reading as the next step in this area.

Feedback 1 ½ years later
Katie tells me that after our constellation she has progressed in her therapy and has had a reading done. She is now working intensively on her self-love process and her rheumatism is slowing getting better.

CASE 8

"I want to develop creatively" - lacking sense of personal identity
Individual constellation

Erin M. is 48 years old, married and has 2 children

Erin is interested in my "inner child" constellation in order to grasp her untapped creative potential. She believes a blockage from her childhood is to blame. She was adopted as a baby and only saw her birth parents once at the age of 30. She tells me about the following incident:

Erin: "I discovered at the age of 16 that I was adopted – not through my adoptive parents, but my teacher. She had a document on her desk which showed that I was adopted. She didn't know that I was unaware of this. It was a shock for me!
Later, when I had my own family, the doorbell rang three times in the same week. Each time I was afraid to open it, even without knowing who was actually outside. The fourth time, I opened the door and saw my birth parents for the first time in my life. My father was suffering from cancer and wanted to make peace with me before he passed on.

I didn't let them in, but rather assured them that their decision to give me up for adoption had been the best one and that my adoptive parents were very loving and cared well for me. I couldn't go any further."

Individual constellation with pillows
Erin places four pillows. It is interesting that she chooses two pillows for herself – a light one and a dark one. One represents the goal of realizing her potential, the other her blockage.

She places her own pillows on top of each other. The pillow for the blockage is directly in front of her and the pillow for the goal is right behind it. She believes that she doesn't need much to reach her goal.

<u>Perception in Erin's position:</u> I sense that I am uncomfortable with the dark pillow and that I can't perceive it as a part of me. I remove it and place it at the side. Through kinesiologic testing I see that this pillow represents a great-uncle from the father's side of the family who probably died as a child. Erin was this child who died in a previous life.

I ask Erin to take her position and speak the following resolution statements to herself:

Resolution statements
Erin to her deceased great-uncle: "You are part of this and have your own space which I cannot enter. You are dead, but I live." She takes this soul, who she was in a previous life, to heart. She then places an additional pillow for his mother (her great-grandmother).

Erin to her great-grandmother: "I now lovingly relinquish the grief for your dead son and the maternal responsibility for him to you. She then lays the great-uncle's pillow next to that of the great-grandmother. Erin now feels liberated.

Erin mentions that her adoptive mother had an abortion. Since dead children are often represented by subsequent living ones, I ask her to place a pillow for this dead child, which testing shows was a girl. She places it on top of the pillow representing the blockage. It's easy to determine that she was intended to replace the aborted daughter for the adoptive parents and felt unable recognize her own self.

I ask Erin to place two additional pillows for her adoptive parents. Once she finds a good place for them, she immediately takes the pillow for the dead child and places it with those of the adoptive parents.

Resolution statements
Erin to her adoptive parents: "Dear parents, I had nothing to do with your dead daughter and I cannot replace her for you. She has her own place, which I now leave with you."

Erin also assumed the maternal role for the dead child, because her adoptive mother could not accept her in her heart because of her guilt.

Erin to her adoptive mother: "You are her mother, not me, and I now leave all responsibility as a mother with you and all of the associated feelings of guilt and sorrow."

The aborted child is not pleased with Erin because she took over its place.
Erin to the dead child: "I'm sorry that you couldn't make it. I am not guilty for this. I cannot take your place – you are the birth child of my adoptive mother, not me. I respect your place. Please look kindly upon me so that I can realize my own life, even if you were unable to realize your own."
These phrases resolve the jealousy of the dead child and Erin can now release herself from this identification.

In order for Erin to now fully and completely realize her goals, she must accept self-responsibility for her life.

Accepting responsibility for one's own life
Erin to her adoptive parents: "Dear mother and father, I thank you for everything. It's all good between us. I now accept responsibility for my life and you are free from it." She senses that something has relaxed in her solar plexus and feels energy beginning to flow in her spine.

Accepting her own identity
Erin tells me that her adoptive parents were very afraid that they would lose their cherished adopted daughter to her birth parents. That's why they gave her the impression that her birth parents were riff-raff. As a result, Erin feels contempt for her birth parents, which she has acquired from her adoptive parents. This contempt hinders her from accepting her real parents' roots and she therefore also feels contempt for herself in her heritage.

Only by accepting our birth parents can we find the way to our own identity!

Resolution statements for accepting our birth parents
Erin to her adoptive parents: "Dear mother, dear father, I now relinquish your contempt for my birth parents to you. My love for you is safe. Please look upon my kindly as I also accept my birth parents into my heart, since I come from them. I thank you." For the first time she feels the ability to turn to her birth parents.

Erin to her birth parents: "Dear parents, I come from you and I thank you for my life. I thank you for giving me the greatest of gifts and leave it at that. I now fully accept responsibility for my life and you are now free from it." Erin can now accept her parents for the first time. I recommend that she repeat these statements several times at home in order to strengthen her roots and thereby her own identity.

Erin now feels very near to her goal. She lays another poster for her inner child down, which contains her creative potential and her entire range of emotions.

Perception in the inner child's position: "I feel very lonely and abandoned. It's the feeling Erin experienced when her birth parents gave her up for adoption. In order to follow through with her own self-love and to give the inner child everything it needs, I ask her to speak the following phrases:

Resolution statements for accepting one's inner child
Erin to her inner child: "Dear Erin, you are the small one and I am big. I now accept responsibility for you and everything that you need. I will never abandon you again, but will always be there for you. You are valuable and important to

me and I love you just as you are. I look forward to all of your feelings, be they sorrow, pain or joy – you can express everything." She takes the inner child's pillow and presses it to her heart and can now progress to her goal. She senses that she can only reach this potential in connection with her inner child. I recommend that she get an inner child puppet and communicate with it every day to find out what exactly it needs. Healing her inner child is a long process, which will now be initiated to let self-love flow again.

Feedback 2 weeks later
Erin calls me: "I feel dynamic and more creative. I activated my ancestors' Feng Shui corner in my home. Oddly enough, an aunt whom I hadn't heard from in 30 years called me! I've already purchased an inner child puppet, which I placed in a highly visible spot in the living room. I believe she's doing well with me. Both my husband and my children have lovingly accepted it. My husband even tucks her in at night."

CASE 9

"I can't orgasm" – a vow of chastity

Group constellation

Antoinette H. is 35 years old, single and has 2 children

Antoinette comes to my seminar with a very intimate topic. Antoinette: "I want to know why I've never had an orgasm during sex. The only way for me to orgasm is when I masturbate alone. Although I've had relationships with several men, it never worked with any of them. Even when I thought that I was on the verge, I was actually still a long way off. My unfulfilled sex life is a problem for me and my partner."

Group constellation
In the constellation, Antoinette assumes her position and chooses a representative for the ability to orgasm and another to represent the blockade.

<u>Representative for the ability to orgasm:</u> "I feel motionless and restrained; I feel absolutely no pleasure. When I turn to the representative for the blockade, I see images from one of Antoinette's previous lives."

Antoinette as a nun in a previous life
I see Antoinette dressed as a nun. She still carries her vows of chastity with her

and doesn't allow herself to experience joy and ecstasy in her sexuality. Beyond that, as a nun she promised only to love God. When I suggest that Antoinette release herself from this old promise, she's not yet ready at first. Antoinette: "Life as a nun offers me safety from the world." With the help of a representative, a number of images from this previous life manifest themselves. As a special bond to the church, it appears that Antoinette had an intimate relationship with a priest. For her, this love for him was an expression of her love for God. A child came about from this romantic relationship. It was immediately taken from her after birth and she had to leave the abbey. She never saw her child again.

<u>Antoinette:</u> Cries and holds a pillow representing her child close to her heart. Only after she has taken her lost child back into her heart can she release herself from her old promises and vows as a nun.

Resolution statements to resolve her previous life as a nun
<u>Antoinette to the church:</u> "I now release myself from the vow to love only God and am now free to love all people. I release myself from my vow of chastity, that I would renounce my body, sexual desire and worldly things in general. I am now open to physical desire, joy and all earthly pleasures. These are all gifts from God and meant for my enjoyment.
I relinquish all doctrines that sexuality and physical desire is something dirty for which I must be ashamed. I relinquish the dogma that sexuality is only meant for procreation. This dogma no longer serves me! I thank you for everything I was able to learn with you as a nun. I now take back all of my power, strength and responsibility that I rendered to you."

Antoinette is relieved. The representative for her ability to orgasm suddenly seems cheerful, lively and full of energy. Antoinette looks at her skeptically and is anxious to see if the constellation will work.

Feedback at a seminar four weeks later
Antoinette: "Today I'm happy to share that the constellation worked. For me it's like a miracle that at 35 years old I was able to experience my first orgasm with my partner. At first I couldn't believe it and thought it might be a one-off thing, but (Antoinette laughs) it really worked.

CASE 10

Being free for your own family – assuming a father's power and strength

Group constellation

Joseph and Anna K. are in their mid-30s, married and have one daughter

Joseph comes together with his wife, Anna, to the group in order to constellate their present family. He wants to know if their one-year-old daughter still carries burdens from her ancestral families.

Group constellation
Joseph places three representatives for his present family in a triangular position. <u>Representative for Joseph:</u> "I don't know exactly which of the two women is my daughter and which is my partner; it's like a love triangle." Even his wife and child do not feel like a family. From a constellation of his ancestral family, I know that Joseph's father divorced his mother and left with another woman. I ask to include his father, his second wife and Joseph's mother in the constellation. He places his mother beside the representative for himself and places his father and his second wife away from everyone else. Joseph's representative stands symbolically exactly between the parents and bears the weight of their failed relationship. It appears that after the divorce, he took on the role of his mother's substitute partner. I attempt to resolve the situation with resolution statements:

Resolution statements for clearing up family dynamics
<u>Joseph to his mother:</u> "I am not your partner and I cannot replace my father for you." His representative has difficulty saying this statement and tells us that he does not want to leave this partnership with his mother. The representative for his mother says: "You're going to abandon me now, too!" (appears desperate). Since no resolution comes about on the family-systemic level between Joseph and his mother, I do kinesiologic testing and recognize a karmic entanglement between the two. I ask Joseph to place a representative for this in the picture.

Assuming a father's power and strength from a previous life
Joseph places a woman to represent the previous life precisely between himself and his mother. The representative seems sad and says: "I'm looking at mounds of rocks, which look like graves." At this moment, the representative for Joseph's mother moves away and takes a place beside the representative for his father. My inner images show that in a previous life, Joseph had the same parents as he does today. His father at that time was a mighty ruler who died young (hence the graves). His son assumed this power and filled the partnership void alongside his mother. It is now clear that there is a relationship pattern this family is re-

peating in the present life. The father leaves and Joseph once again takes his place alongside his mother.

For the mother's representative, this entanglement was resolved when the image of her then-husband's grave appeared. She now knows who her husband and son are and can let go of Joseph. There is still a cleft in Joseph's relationship with his father, who still appears very small in comparison to Joseph. I have him speak the following resolution statements:

Resolution statements to clarify a previous life

Joseph to his father: "Dear father, I now return all of your power, which I still carry for you, back to you. I will now go with my own power." At first hesitant as to whether he should release the fathers' power, he then gets the feeling that he does possess sufficient power of his own to stand on his own two feet in this life. The father seems relieved and has increased in stature. Joseph can now accept him as his father.

Joseph to his parents: "What didn't go right between you two has nothing to do with me; I leave that now with you – I am only the child." Joseph is now free for his own family. Joyfully he hugs his wife, Anna.

Feedback one year later

Joseph tells me that he's happy with his family and that they've just had a son. He no longer feels any burdens associated with his daughter. Joseph describes his relationship with his father as very good.

His relationship with his mother is somewhat more distanced, but harmonious.

CASE 11

Love that wasn't allowed to be – Russian melancholy

Group constellation

Anna L., 28 years old, single, no children

During the seminar, Anna wants to explore a topic that's been weighing on her for some time. Anna: "I'm not sure where all this sadness in me originates. I immediately start crying at the slightest occasion and sentimentality has become a part of my life. I want more love in my life! In particular, I want to improve my relationship with my mother. I can't really get close to her."

Group constellation

In the group, Anna constellates her mother's side of her ancestral family. In her parents' constellation, her mother stands completely to the side and doesn't feel a part of the family. When we include her mother's first husband, who left her, we see that Anna is her mother's substitute for him, that she thereby has taken on the role of the substitute partner. Furthermore, she carries her mother's feelings towards him. Because of this entanglement, Anna has often borne the brunt of her mother's frustrations, which were actually directed towards her first husband.

Resolution statements

Anna to her mother: "Dear mama, I had nothing to do with your first husband and I cannot be a substitute for him. I lovingly return to you all of the anger, disappointment and grief that I've carried for you."

The representative for her mother begins to sob; Anna's representative goes to comfort her. The hex has been broken; mother and daughter can now find each other again.

In further constellations with her maternal ancestors, a family secret emerges: Anna's maternal grandmother seems anxious and nervous in her role and appears to be keeping a secret. When we add her husband, Anna's grandfather, tests tell me that he is not the biological father of Anna's mother. When we position another person for her biological father, we detect the grandmother's great love for a Russian, who fathered Anna's mother during the Russian occupation of Austria. When he appears, the grandmother looks away and becomes even more nervous. Anna is very moved and feels a strong connection with the Russian. She stands in his place and bears his sadness and sentimentality over the love that wasn't allowed to be. She also carries a feeling of forbidden love from her grandmother.

Resolution statements
Anna to her grandmother: "Dear grandma, I'm sorry that your love wasn't allowed to exist. I now leave all the associated feelings of forbidden love and your subsequent sadness with you. I have nothing to do with your great love and I cannot replace it for you. I now leave him in your heart." The grandmother takes back her feelings and can look at her Russian love for the first time. Her eyes are beaming with joy and she seems relieved.

Grandmother to Anna: "Dear Anna, you have nothing to do with my love and you are now free from it. Even if my love was forbidden, yours may now thrive!" Anna hugs her grandmother tightly.

Anna to her grandmother's Russian lover: "You are my biological grandfather. You are part of the family and are the only real father for my mother. You now have your own place in our family and I no longer need to stand in your place. I lovingly return all your feelings for my grandmother, your sadness and sentimentality; they belong to you and not to me."
They hug each other.

We add the country of Russia to the constellation and Anna enthusiastically accepts an additional ancestral homeland. Anna: "I've always identified with the Russian mentality and I love their music and passion!"

Connection to a previous life
During kinesiologic testing, I see that Anna had a forbidden love for a Russian in a previous life. This explains why she connected with the failed love of her grandparents and experienced the breakdown of her relationship with her mother. Due to the ancestral entanglements, she was able to perceive feelings from her previous life and thereby heal them. Her love can now flow again and thrive.

Feedback one year later
Anna: "I hardly feel any sadness or melancholy any more; every once in a while just a little. My relationship with my mother has become very good. We are getting closer and she's expressing her love for me as best she can. I recently found a partner with whom I'm very happy. My love can finally spread its wings."

CASE 12

My husband won't take responsibility for himself

Remote constellation
Iris and Ben K. are around 40 years old, married and have four children

Iris calls me in desperation and asks me to do an urgent remote constellation for her. Iris: "Recently my husband and I keep butting heads. I have to do everything myself – even what's actually his responsibility. I don't want to any longer and want to know why he doesn't bear his responsibility himself."

Remote constellation with blocks – Ben as Iris' son in a previous life
I see the following image in the block constellation: I recognize a previous life in which Iris' current husband, Ben, was her son. She had an abortion, since the father didn't want to assume his parental responsibilities. Although she could have raised the child alone, she placed all of the responsibility on the father and blamed him alone for the abortion.

Consequences on Iris' current life
The result is that Iris overloads herself with responsibility not properly her own in order to make up for her lack of it in this previous life. Furthermore, she also tries to compensatewith a motherly role towards Ben in this life due to her feelings of guilt. That's why she assumes the role of a substitute for Ben's mother in this life.

Resolution statements for a previous life
Iris to Ben's then-father: "I now accept my part of all the guilt and responsibility I placed on you at the time for our son's abortion and leave you only with your part."
Iris to her then-son (today her husband, Ben): "I accept my former responsibility for you as a mother and admit that I didn't want to bring you into the world alone. I now expect you to take responsibility for having chosen me as a mother in this experience. I now release myself from all feelings of guilt towards you."

Resolution statements for current life
Iris to mother-in-law: "You are the only real mother for Ben, not me. I now leave all maternal responsibility for Ben with you."
Iris to Ben: "Dear Ben, I am no longer your mother and you are no longer my son. You are a man. I now give you back responsibility for your life."

Power and dignity
During kinesiologic testing, I recognize that Iris is not yet ready to return Ben's

power and dignity as a man and thus allow him to fully and completely accept his responsibilities. In the constellation with the blocks, I see another life as a hindrance.

Ben and Iris as partners in a previous life
Ben was at that time a woman, a black magic sorceress, and Iris was incarnated as a man. Ben was very interested in him, but could only gain him as a partner through manipulation and sorcery.

Effects on Iris and Ben's current relationship
Today's effect is that Iris still carries old fears of Ben's power and strength. That's why she doesn't want to grant him entitlement. She can release herself from these old fears and entanglements with the following resolution statements.

Resolution statements to resolve a previous life
Iris to Ben: "Dear Ben, I now agree to my learning experiences with you, of being a victim of your power struggles and can accept my part of the responsibility for this. I now take back the power and dignity, which I once relinquished to you. I return all of the power and dignity as a man, which I took from you in fear. We are both equally strong and equally powerful!"

Testing shows no further blockages and I end the remote constellation.

Debriefing:
After the constellation I call Iris and share my images and resolution statements with her. She seems relieved on the telephone. They are about to go on holiday with each other and she wanted to resolve these troublesome entanglements beforehand.

Feedback six months later
Iris: "I've experienced a significant change between Ben and myself. When I was recently confronted with bank issues that affected both of us, I told him, "You'll have to take care of this – it's too much for me." Since then Ben has taken care of many things that I previously had to do alone. I can now expect him to accept responsibility and have faith that he can do it without me."

CASE 13

"Careful during sex!" – fear of accepting the masculine

Individual constellation

Andrea S. is 35 years old, married and has no children

Andrea comes to me for an individual session to see about her inhibited sex life with her husband. Andrea: "Although I like feeling my husband inside me, at the same time I feel a vaginal tightness that makes intercourse difficult."

Block constellation
Andrea positions a block for herself, one for her husband and one for the sexual blockage (feeling of tightness) between them. I test and determine that it is not her own blockage which is impairing her sex life, but rather an assumed issue from her maternal grandmother. After Andrea positions her grandmother in the constellation, we see that she has acquired a doctrine from her grandmother that having sex with a man is dangerous due to the possibility of contracting STDs. In her grandmother's time during the war, many women were raped during the Russian occupation and such a belief was an expedient protective measure.

Resolution statements
<u>Andrea to her grandmother:</u> "I'm sorry that for you sexuality was associated with so many dangers and that for you it was so dangerous to let a man enter you. I now leave all of the fears associated with sexuality behind with you. I'm now safe, grandma, and I can now devote myself with confidence to my partner."

When I examine this kinesiologically, I see that Andrea is not yet free from her grandmother's sexual blockage. I recognize that her grandmother has promised to keep this doctrine as a source of protection.

Dissolving the promise
<u>Andrea to her grandmother:</u> "I now release myself from the promise of your doctrine that it is dangerous to let a man enter me. I now leave this belief and all of the associated fears with you."
Now Andrea is free from external influences upon her sexuality.

Andrea as a prostitute in a previous life
Within the context of this systemic entanglement, the constellation shows that in a previous life, Andrea was a prostitute and lived in constant fear of contracting diseases from her clients. It is the same fear of sex with new partners which the grandmother also carried into this life. By identifying with her grandmother,

she is able to gain cognizance of this old issue and release herself from it with the resolution statements.

Feedback four months later
Andrea: "I'm so grateful for the ability to be open for intercourse with my husband. I now feel how I release myself to him and how we flow together. It's a beautiful feeling."

CASE 14

A) "I'm invisible" – the brother who died in infancy

Group constellation
Isabella M. is 38 years old, divorced and the mother of one son

Isabella, in the presence of her mother, constellates her ancestral family in the group. The goal of her constellation is to have success in her love life. After a divorce, she is now together with a partner, but isn't yet comfortable moving in together with him. In her ancestral family's constellation, the following image appears:

Isabella's representative: "I feel like nobody takes notice of me; I'm invisible!" She is identifying with her younger brother, Edward. At seven months old, he stopped breathing and died suddenly. Isabella found him dead and was extremely shocked. Subconsciously she carries her parents' feeling of guilt for the death of her brother. Since this stroke of fate, her parents were focused on Edward in the grave and not on Isabella.

Resolution statements
Isabella to Edward: "My dear brother, you are part of the family and have a place that I cannot replace. I will stop filling that void and leave the masculine with you. You have perished, but I live."

Isabella's representative initially finds it difficult to take her place in life, since she perceives life as something threatening. (See Case 14B)
Edward to Isabella: "Dear sister, you are not guilty for my death. It was my path to go and yours to stay. I give you my blessing, that you may have a good life."

Isabella to her parents: "Dear mom and dad, I leave you with your responsibility for my brother, Edward, and all of the feelings of guilt associated with his death. You are the parents, I am just the child."

Isabella's mother is very moved and begins to cry. She sees that she has paid far too little attention to her daughter and lovingly hugs her.

B) The masculine threat – perpetrator and victim

When we position Isabella's maternal grandparents in the picture, we see that her grandmother was raped by three Russians during the war. Isabella identifies with her and carries her feelings of powerlessness, shame and the remembrance of having suffered abuse.

She subconsciously perceives the male threat which her grandmother experienced.

Parallel to one of Isabella's previous lives as a perpetrator
During testing, it appears that Isabella herself was one of the Russians who had raped her grandmother at the time. To counteract this, today she identifies with the feelings of the victim.

Resolution statements
Isabella to her grandmother: "Dear grandmother, I'm sorry for what happened to you. I honor and respect your difficult fate and now lovingly leave it with you." I let Isabella represent herself in the constellation. She bows deeply in front of her grandmother.

I ask Isabella now to take the three Russians also to heart. Once she understands that she herself was one of the perpetrators, it will help her to take back this dissociated facet of her personality, which she has projected onto men as a threatening quality, and move past this one-sided victim mentality. Isabella now also takes the perpetrators to heart and says: "Everything feels peaceful now."
In order for Isabella's love to prosper, we also ask her maternal grandparents and great-grandparents for their blessings, since both pairs were divorced.

Resolution statements
Isabella to her grandparents and great-grandparents: "I'm sorry that your love didn't succeed and I now leave all of the associated feelings with you. Please give me your blessings, that my love may now grow and thrive. I thank you." Isabella senses how kindly they look upon her and wish the best for her.

For Isabella, the greatest gift is that of being recognized by her parents and her new ability to find a good place for herself in life. This esteemed position in the family also affords a good place for her partnership and career.

Feedback eight months later

Isabella: "I split up with my last partner and am currently single. I hope that this will change soon, however. People tell me that I seem happier and more energetic and I feel more open towards others. My relationship with my mother has become more relaxed. She is giving me my space, which I find very comfortable.

CASE 15

Doubts about fatherhood – an insecure identity

Remote constellation

Janet A. is 44 years old, divorced and has three children

Janet has been divorced for a year and a half, but still works at her ex-husband's company. She'd like to find a new partner and has already met two interesting men.

Janet: "In the beginning everything is wonderful. I believe to have found the ideal partner and that the feeling is mutual. However, shortly thereafter both of the men I was dating backed out because they weren't yet ready to be in a new relationship. We talked many times about the source of their insecurities, but ultimately neither of them stayed with me. I feel like a guidepost for the men I meet. When am I finally going to find one who stays with me?"

Remote constellation with blocks

I position a block for Janet, one for her ex-husband and for the two men with whom she wanted a relationship, respectively. Testing showed that Janet's ex-husband Brad had not yet let her go and was blocking her new relationships. I recognize a contract of the soul for this life, in which Janet and Brad had intended to remain together to the end. Brad and Janet did not reach the decision to separate easily. They tried various counseling services to save their marriage. Ultimately, Janet realized that her husband was unable to develop further and that he impeded her own personality development. It was very difficult for Brad to accept that their marriage was really over.

Dissolving a contract of the soul

Janet to Brad: "Dear Brad, I hereby release both of us from our contract of the soul, to be partners and stay by each another's side for the rest our lives. This old agreement is no longer right for me, since I am unable develop together with you."

I test to see if Janet is now free for a new relationship, but there is still a blockage to a new partnership. In the block constellation, I see that the blockage is tied to her lack of self-identity. Since I had already constellated Janet's ancestral family, I know that her mother was always unsure as to who Janet's biological father was. At the time Janet was conceived, she had sexual relationships with her then-fiancée, Arthur, and her future husband, George. Janet's mother always told her that after the pregnancy she had feelings only for George and was no longer interested in Arthur. However, Janet's grandmother said that she looked like Arthur's family and not like George at all. Janet also never really got on well with George. They often fought and she always felt resentment from him. Janet has worked on this issue intensively. A spiritual medium assured her that her life line clearly went to George as her biological father, just like her younger sister, Jana. Nevertheless, she never felt 100% sure about her paternal heritage.

Remote constellation with blocks
I position blocks representing Janet, her mother, the fiancé Arthur and George. Testing shows that George is definitely Janet's biological father. However, Janet still carries her mother's doubt that she may be Arthur's child. This doubt destabilizes her self-identity and hinders her from fully accepting her biological father. Her father, George, has also acquired this doubt from her mother and cannot completely accept his daughter as his child. The result is that both quarrel often and that Janet's younger sister, Jana, was preferred by their father. We will remove all doubt with the following statements.

Resolution statements to resolve self-identity
Janet to her mother and grandmother: "Dear mom and grandma, I now relinquish your doubts as to whether George is my father. Jana and I have the same father and I now completely accept him into my heart as my father!"

Janet to her father: "Dear dad, I also relinquish your insecurities that I could be someone else's child. You are my real father and you may now accept me as your daughter. I take you to heart as my father. I am both like and unlike you and accept my heritage from you."

I recommend that Janet now breathe deeply and fully accept her father.

Janet to her parents: "Dear mom and dad, you are the right parents for me. Please give me your blessings so that I can enter into a fruitful relationship. I thank you."
I now ask Janet to imagine being hugged by both of her parents and to take them to heart. After formulating the resolution statements, I test to determine that Janet can now integrate her true identity. Only by accepting her biological father is her heart open for the right partner.

Feedback five months later

Janet is happy! She's in a new partnership with Ralph, who complements her very well.

Janet: "At first I wasn't attracted at all to Ralph. He's a smoker and likes to drink. In the beginning, that bothered me a lot. I had a mental picture of my future partner and he didn't fit in at all. Since I've gotten to know him better, I've changed my mind. I can only recommend that people move past first impressions and get to know people, because otherwise you might reject your dream partner at first glance."

CASE 16

My sister's jealousy – unequal inheritance

Remote constellation

Mona S. is 39 years old, married and has one son

One week after constellating her ancestral family, Mona calls me.
Mona: "I've finally found my place in my family, but I'm still having problems with Katherine, my sister, who is very jealous of me. She is always competing for my father's attention. I get the feeling that she'd rather me not even be there. My paternal grandmother always preferred Katherine over me and when she died my sister inherited everything and I was left empty-handed."

To determine what must be resolved between Mona and her sister, I conduct a remote constellation.

Remote constellation
I position a block for Mona, one for her sister and one for her father. Since I don't recognize any family systemic entanglements, I test a former life as the culprit and place an additional block representing it. I then see the following image:

Mona was a priest in a previous life
Mona was a male evangelical priest with his own family. Katherine was his daughter at the time. Her paternal grandmother in this life was his wife at that time. I see that Mona as a priest is wholeheartedly devoted to the church. When she died young of illness, the majority of the inheritance went to the church and not to the family she'd left behind. The wife and daughter felt betrayed and were very angry about this.

Consequences for Mona in this life:
To balance her karma, Mona must face financial punishment from her grandmother, to whom she still owes an inheritance from a previous life.

Resolution statements to resolve her former life as a priest
Mona to her sister and grandmother in her present life: "I accept my share of the responsibility for depriving you of your inheritance. I'm sorry. I now leave your share of the responsibility for this experience with you. I hereby release myself from these old feelings of indebtedness to you. Everything is square between us."

Katherine's jealousy of Mona is still not resolved. The block constellation shows me yet another life between the two.

Mona and Katherine were sisters in a previous life
Mona and Katherine were previously sisters, but Katherine was the elder of the two. They had the same father as today. Their mother at that time is the paternal grandmother in their present family. The parents' relationship is not one of love. The mother has a lover and the father is very angry about this. Due to the parents' strained relationship, a wedge is driven between the children because Mona is close to her father and Katherine to her mother. When the father died, he left his entire fortune to Mona. I see jewelry, especially rings that Mona inherited from him. The mother and Katherine are left with nothing. Today, Katherine is still jealous of the connection Mona had to their father in the former life. Although Mona is not responsible for the preferential treatment, she still bears the feelings of guilt from her former parents.

Resolution statements to resolve the previous life as sisters
Mona to her father: "Dear father, I now relinquish your feelings of guilt and responsibility towards my sister because you penalized her with your love and estate. I am not at fault."

Mona to her former mother (today's grandmother): As my former mother, you are responsible for the wedge driven between my sister and me. I now leave this responsibility and associated feelings of guilt with you. Neither Katherine nor I are to blame for what went wrong between you and father. I accept only my part of the responsibility in choosing to have this experience with you as my parents."

Mona to Katherine: "Dear sister, I'm sorry that my father preferred me over you. I am not to blame for that. You have to work that out yourself with dad. We can share him alike. I am his second and you his third daughter. Each of us may now receive what is rightfully ours."

During testing, I see yet another karmic entanglement between them, but it is not yet ready to be resolved.

Feedback three months later
Mona: "At my partner's behest, I called my sister to wish her a happy birthday. She was very excited to hear from me and invited us to her daughter's baptism two days later. I was amazed that the family gathering went so smoothly."

CASE 17

Physical pain as an offset for guilt

Individual constellation

Oscar F. is 44 years old, single and has no children

Oscar comes to me for an individual constellation in order to determine the cause of the acute pain he's had for fifteen years. The pain began in his shoulders and in recent years has spread to his arms and legs.

Oscar: "I used to be a healthy and productive man. I suddenly started having pain and it kept getting stronger. I can't give 100% at work anymore and my girlfriend left me because I could no longer physically fulfill her needs. I'm afraid of getting too involved with my current girlfriend because I may not be able to satisfy her, either."

Constellation with blocks
Oscar positions a blue block for himself, a large yellow one for his father, whom he remembers as being very aggressive, and a small yellow doll for his mother. He stacks three large, red blocks on top of one another to represent his pain and places them on his own blue block.

Through testing, I recognize that Oscar bears this pain from his paternal grandfather. He doesn't really remember him, because his grandfather moved to another state after separating from his grandmother. I see that even after marrying Oscar's grandfather, his grandmother's heart always remained with her first love.

Oscar bears his grandfather's feelings of resentment and sadness towards his wife's first love because he could never really win over her heart. Furthermore, he fills the void left by his grandfather's father, Oscar's great-grandfather, about whom Oscar knows nothing. No one ever spoke about him.

Resolution statements
Oscar to his great grandfather: "You are part of the family and are the only father for my grandfather, not me. I now leave your fatherly responsibilities for him with you."

Oscar to his grandfather: "I am not your father; I am your grandson. I now relinquish the responsibility for your life, power and dignity as a man and father. Grandpa, I'm sorry that your love for grandma didn't work out. I now release all of your feelings of anger and sadness towards her first love; I have nothing to do with it."

Subsequent testing showed that neither entanglement could be resolved. I see that a previous life must first be resolved.

Oscar as a priest in a former life
I ask Oscar to place another block to represent what is needed for resolution. He places a large blue block some distance away and says, "This should be far away from the rest." In this blue block I see one of Oscar's previous lives as a Protestant pastor. His great-grandfather in this life was then a kitchen maid in the parsonage and his grandfather was one of the 15 children he had with her. Although he was allowed to marry, he remained single. When Oscar placed a green block to represent the reason for this, I see Oscar's great love for God. He was unable to appreciate or love the mother of his children and treated her disrespectfully. When he died young, a majority of his estate went to the church and not to his family. His lover (his great-grandfather today) was very angry about his disregard for his family.

Consequences for Oscar's current life
Today he still bears feelings of guilt towards the former mother of his children. That's why he bears his grandfather's anger and sadness surrounding his failed relationship. This correlates to the experiences of his former lover, whose love he did not recognize or requite.

Resolution statements for the previous life
Oscar to his former mistress (today's great-grandfather): "I'm sorry that I could not give you my love and appreciation back then. My heart was solely reserved for God. I now give you my respect as my lover and mother of our fifteen children. I accept my share of the responsibility for my behavior towards you and relinquish your share for choosing this experience with me. I release myself from all feelings of guilt towards you."

I test and determine that Oscar is still blocked from resolving his guilty conscience towards his former mistress. He wants to blame it on the church, since that's where he vowed "to love only God."

<u>Oscar to the church:</u> "I accept my responsibility for choosing to vow, of my own free will, to love only God. Since it no longer serves me today, I now release myself from it."

Oscar can finally accept his responsibility for his former actions. The previous life had to be resolved first in order to resolve the family systemic entanglements with his present grandfather and great-grandfather (see resolutions statements above). I recommend that Oscar partake in kinesiologic sessions in addition to his medical treatments to dissipate the pain memory he has built up over the years.

Feedback one year later
Oscar: "For a short while, the pain was better. After your constellation I still did pain therapy, which resulted in almost three pain-free months. A couple of months later my pain had moved from above to below; I now feel it all in my legs. I was on the go a lot - perhaps I overexerted myself. At work I'm active again and I'm really enjoying that."
I recommend that Oscar come to me for another constellation to determine the cause of this wandering pain.

CASE 18

"I feel guilty - I failed!" – a separation

Individual constellation
Oscar F. is 44 years old, single and has no children

Three months after our last individual constellation (see Case 17), Oscar comes to me with another issue. Oscar and his girlfriend Sandra separated a few days ago. He's very sad about this and wants to take a closer look at why the relationship failed. Oscar and Sandra lived together in her apartment. Recently, he couldn't do anything right by her and she asked him to move out. When he did move out, Sandra began to cry and said that she was solely responsible for the whole situation.
Oscar: "She treated me very badly. She always had something to criticize me for and did so in front of other people - it was really embarrassing. She spoke to me as if I were a little child and accused me of being unable to make decisions. She gave me the feeling that I did everything wrong."

Resolution statements to resolve this previous life
Since Oscar has assumed responsibility for things over which he had no control

over in former times, I ask him to take a seat at his pillow and say the following statements to Beatrice: Oscar to Beatrice: "I'm sorry for what you suffered at that time. I would gladly have helped save your son from his death. However, I was unable to do anything; I was helpless. I now relinquish your fate and the accompanying pain. It belongs to you and not to me."

Subsequent testing shows that Oscar is not yet ready to return the responsibility to Beatrice. The next step is to resolve the emotional trauma resulting from his guilt and failure. This time around, I recommend that he find a kinesiologist to help him resolve these feelings. Oscar agrees. He can now see that the relationship with Sandra revealed a deep wound in him that requires healing.

Feedback one year later
Oscar's voice sound strong on the telephone. Oscar: "I had two more sessions with the kinesiologist you recommended and we were able to resolve several old feelings. Soon thereafter I broke up with Sandra. I was very disappointed in how she treated me. Six months later I met my current girlfriend. She's a very kind woman and I feel very happy with her."

CASE 19

"I'll protect you, mama!" - No one else will care for my mother

Remote constellation per telephone

Angelica F. is 38 years old, married and has three children

Angelica calls me in a state of despair. "I'm so angry I'm about to explode. I have to do something! You know that I've been caring for my mother for three months now. Although it's difficult, I'm glad to do it for her. She was always there for us - she watched my children and my sibling's children when we were away. If she hadn't been there, we wouldn't have been able to enjoy a vacation. The problem is that I am the only one of my four siblings willing to take care of our mother. I get the feeling that they don't care if she's at home, in a nursing home or already dead. My sister always says, "I just don't know how you do it. I'd be at my wit's end by now. I feel very hurt when I hear that and it makes me very angry. Our mother has earned more respect than that!"

I interrupt Angelica: "While you were speaking, I saw images of you and your mother. You were lying with your arms around her in a protective position and wouldn't let anyone near her."

I test and see a previous life.

Angelica as her mother's guardian in a previous life
Angelica's mother was also her mother in a previous life and she had the same siblings as today. The mother was also very sick and needed care then. Back then, her siblings could hardly wait for her to die in order to get their inheritance. They would gladly have helped their mother die even sooner. Angelica is the only one her mother can trust. Angelica gave her a promise to protect her from the others and to care for her until her death.

Effects on Angelica's current life
Angelica subconsciously still carries this fear that her siblings could do harm to their mother and feels the need to protect her from them. That's why today she still won't let anyone near her mother in that she appears to be the only one prepared to care for their mother. No one besides her feels responsible for their mother.

Angelica speaks the following resolutions statements on the telephone

<u>Angelica to her mother:</u> "Dear mama, I now release myself from the promise to protect you from all the others and to be your sole guardian until your death. You are safe!"

<u>Angelica to her siblings:</u> "Mama is now safe with you. I now relinquish your responsibility, power and dignity to you so that you can be there for her."

I suggest that Angelica make space for her siblings in that she should imagine inviting everyone to visit their mother. Angelica already feels greatly relieved during the first resolution statements. Angelica: "I feel as though a great weight is gone from my chest. The anger has also completely disappeared."

Feedback two days later
Angelica calls to thank me again. Her attitude to her siblings has totally changed and her resentment towards them is gone. She also has a relaxed relationship with her mother. She no longer feels the need to be the only one responsible for their mother.

Individual constellation with pillows
I suggest that Oscar and I do a constellation to determine the causes and ask him to position a pillow for himself and one for Sandra. He lays these diagonally across from each other on the floor.

<u>Perception at Oscar's position:</u> "I feel that something is pulling me back; it feels like a rope dragging me into the past. When I look at Sandra's pillow, I see a fire

that conjures up images of hell. When I observe this for a longer period, I recognize that it's like a self-inflicted punishment; she's a self-imposed hell."

I ask Oscar to place a pillow representing the cause of this self-punishment. He places the pillow a short distance behind him to the left.

Perception in Oscar's position: "In the new pillow I see a woman. She's full of rage, screaming and making scathing gestures towards Sandra."

Since Oscar has no idea who this woman could be, I do kinesiologic testing that points to Oscar's ex-girlfriend, Beatrice. Oscar can't imagine that Beatrice could be angry at Sandra. He and Beatrice have been separated for a long time and have become good friends. A test indicates that this rage has to do with a previous life and I ask Oscar to place an additional pillow representing this. Oscar places a pillow directly in front of his own.

Oscar suffered through war in a previous life

Perception of the previous life: "I see images of war. There are smoldering fires; a battle has ended and there are many dead bodies on the ground. Oscar is one of the defeated soldiers who managed to survive this battle. I see Sandra sitting on a horse. She was male at this time and a victorious enemy soldier. Beatrice was a woman and belonged to the same group as Oscar. When I delve deeper into the images from this battlefield, I see the following scenes: Oscar must stand by as Sandra kills Beatrice's son, a young soldier, before her eyes. Oscar feels helpless; he no longer has a weapon and cannot help the boy. The pain of this desperate mother is deeply engraved into his soul. He feels guilty for being unable to do anything. He'd rather have borne Beatrice's pain than to watch helplessly as her son was killed.

Negative impression

During subsequent testing, I see that Oscar has developed the following impression of himself from this experience: "I am guilty; I am a lame duck."

Consequences for his current life

Oscar encounters Sandra in this life with these internalized feelings of guilt. As punishment for his former failure, he allows her to mistreat and berate him. With her criticism, she reinforces his inner impression of himself that "I am a failure."

CASE 20

"We can't get close to one another" – forbidden love

Individual session

Diane G. is 39 years old, divorced and has one son

I meet Diane at a group meeting with friends of mine involved in energy and life coaching. We discuss our experiences and issues. Diane wants to work with me to analyze the following issue.

Diane: "I've been together with Michael for two months. We're happy together, but every time we start to get close there's a sudden disconnect between us. We subsequently fight and often don't talk to each other for a longer period of time. It's such a shame that our closeness keeps crumbling."

Since I don't have any blocks with me, I ask my inner perception to show me the causes behind this dynamic. The following images from one of Michael and Diane's past lives appear:

Diane and Michael were Native Americans in a previous life – forbidden love

I see Diane and Michael as Native Americans sitting in a tent. They approach each other intimately and are completely in love. Others suddenly storm into the tent. They angrily tear the two apart and drag them outside. At first I don't understand the images, but then I see that Diane and Michael are not from the same tribe. They must keep their love secret because their fathers have already promised them to other partners.

Effects on Diane's relationship with Michael today

Diane and Michael still subconsciously sense the prohibition on their love. This always comes up when they become close and intimate. That's why they are continually unable to remain close.

Resolution statements to resolve their previous lives

<u>Diane to her former father:</u> "Dear father, I now take back the power and self-determination as a woman that I relinquished to you as your daughter. Today I may act of my own free will. I can choose my own partner. I am now free from your forbiddance to love Michael; it is not part of my current life.

<u>Diane to Michael:</u> "Dear Michael, we were not allowed to be together in former times. Today we are free to have a relationship. I allow myself to love you, and you may also love me."

Feedback three months later
Diane tells me that after our individual constellation, she was able to get closer to Michael. Only after Michael participated in a spiritual reading could they totally open up to one another. Sometimes there are several layers to examine in order to completely resolve an issue.

CASE 21

"I have to sacrifice my life for the relationship" – the harem wife in servitude

Remote constellation per telephone

Sylvia K. is 52 years old, single and has no children.

Sylvia is exasperated and calls to explain the following issue to me.

Sylvia: "I recently met Greg, a very interesting man - it was love at first sight. I should be happy, but when I think about getting involved with him I become sad and have a fear of giving up my own life for him."

Initially I'm puzzled by her statements and do kinesiologic testing to see if this feeling stems from this life. It appears to come from one of Sylvia's previous lives. The following images appear to me:

Sylvia as a wife in a harem in a previous life with Greg
I see Sylvia in Egypt in the midst of a large harem. She's not just any wife there – she is Greg's favorite wife and serves him with much love and devotion. Her only task is to be beautiful and be there whenever he needs her.

Effects of Sylvia's former life on her present one
Sylvia associates Greg with the idea of servitude and sacrificing her own life. Since Sylvia has led a productive life with many interests and friends, the idea of giving everything up creates feelings of sadness and fear. I explain that these feelings are not from this life and that she can let them go.

Resolution statements to resolve her previous life as a harem wife
Sylvia to Greg: "I now dissolve all the promises I made as a wife in your harem: my promise to serve and belong only to you, to abstain from my own life and other men, to love and always be there for you. I release you from this former contract stipulating responsibility for me. I take back responsibility over my life

as well as the power and dignity as a woman that I relinquished to you. I belong only to myself - I choose my own partner and path in life." After Sylvia speaks the resolution statements on the telephone she is very relieved.

Feedback
Sylvia calls me two days later to thank me. Sylvia: My fear of sacrificing my life for the relationship is completely gone. I now feel able to have a happy and fulfilling relationship with Greg.

CASE 22

"My fear of my boss" – old feelings of guilt towards my father

Group constellation

Cassandra S. is 28 years old, single and has no children

Cassandra tells the group: "I'm planning on quitting my current job within the next few months because I got a better offer, but I'm already having pangs of fear about how my boss will react. I'm afraid that he'll reject my severance pay claims and that I'll be unable to stand up to him. The constellation shows that Cassandra has a conflict with her father that is similar to the one with her boss. I therefore ask her to constellate herself, her boss and her father.

Group constellation
In the constellation, Cassandra's representative immediately retreats away from her boss. She's unable to approach him as an equal. She turns to the father and says, "Papa, can't you please take care of this matter with my boss, just one more time?" The father declines with a smile.

Cassandra has not yet taken responsibility for her life. She has taken the place of her father's mother and therefore feels responsible for him. That's why she's unable to take responsibility for her own life.

Resolution statements
Cassandra's representative to her father: "Dear papa, I cannot replace your mother. She is the only mother for you, not me. I now relinquish responsibility for your life as well as your power and dignity as a man and a father." Her father retreats from this responsibility; he doesn't want to accept it.
Cassandra's representative also describes difficulty in relinquishing her father's responsibility.

Subsequent testing shows that the situation between them cannot be resolved on the family systemic level. My testing determines that the cause stems from a previous life and I ask Cassandra to position a pillow for it.

Cassandra as her father's mother in a previous life
In this new pillow, I recognize one of Cassandra's previous lives as her father's mother; he was formerly her son. I see that she is unable to care for him and that the father is nowhere to be found. Cassandra's representative sees only blood in the pillow and seems very depressed. As I delve deeper into the picture, I see that Cassandra killed her son in desperation because she was unable to provide for him.

Consequences for her current life
Cassandra still bears strong feelings of guilt towards her father and wants play the motherly role she was unable to in the former life. This is the reason for the difficulty in relinquishing responsibility for his life and recognizing his strength as a father.

Resolution statements to resolve the previous life
Cassandra's representative to her father: "Dear papa, I'm sorry for what I did to you back then – it was terrible! I now accept my share of the responsibility for having killed you. I relinquish your responsibility for having chosen me as your mother." Cassandra's representative is very relieved and her father can now easily accept his responsibility. I test and see that Cassandra's guilt from this former life is now completely absolved.
When I ask her to relinquish responsibility for his life and his power and acknowledge his dignity as a man and a father, the statements flow like water. Cassandra can assume responsibility over herself from her father:

Cassandra's representative to her father: "Dear papa, thank you for everything! I now accept responsibility for my life - you are free." Cassandra's representative grows in power and strength with this statement. She also feels confident enough to discuss these issues with her boss.
Her boss' representative also says, "There's an entirely different dynamic between us!" He also feels her newly-gained strength. When Cassandra assumes her own place, she feels strong and doesn't have a grain of fear in issuing her termination notice and asserting her claims to a severance package.

Feedback six months later
Cassandra: "I'm no longer afraid of my boss. He has his own ideas about how I should do my work, but I no longer let him manipulate me. Since the constellation, I've been able to assert myself much better. The other job offer is still on the table, but it will be a while before it becomes final."

CASE 23

Longing for and rejection of Jesus

Individual constellation
Andrea L. is 38 years old, in a relationship and has no children

Andrea comes to analyze the reason why she can't let go of her ex-boyfriend, John, and doesn't feel free for her current partner, Roland.

Andrea: "I had a very spiritual connection with John. When we met, first our souls, then our hearts and soon thereafter also our bodies merged into a single entity. He was the first man who introduced me to the Bible and brought me closer to Jesus. Our sexuality was like a prayer to God - we melted into one body. We separated because he felt attracted to other women and wasn't prepared for a steady relationship. It took many years for me to get over him. Recently I feel like I can't find my way to Jesus without him. It seems the only possible way is with him."

Block constellation
Andrea positions a block for herself, for John and for Jesus. Her own block stands away from the other two. She longs to feel connected to Jesus, but can't find her way. When we place another block to represent what is lacking, it reveals Mary Magdalene. Andrea begins to beam and places Jesus next to Mary Magdalene. It is suddenly clear to her that she cannot accept the one-sided exaltation of a male god; she can't accept Jesus without the feminine dimension. Now her notion of God is complete and veritable. She senses a great antagonism towards the church and blames them for the repression of femininity! When we add the institution of the church, we see that in her former life as a cardinal Andrea had eliminated the feminine from her notion of God. She now understands why as a woman she feels a need to fight for her place in the church. She now accepts responsibility for her actions with the following resolution statements:

Resolution statements to resolve her previous and current lives
Andrea to the church: "I was also one of you and helped to eliminate feminine power and strength from the church. I now accept my share of the responsibility for my former actions." Andrea must still release herself from her former vows in order to accept her feminine divine channel again.

Andrea to the church: "I now release myself from the vow to serve only the male divine channel, Jesus Christ, the only son of God. I now allow myself to recognize the feminine side of God again." Andrea looks joyfully to Mary Magdalene.

Andrea to Mary Magdalene: "You are part of the holy family! I am only complete with you. I recognize you as the feminine channel of God. Andrea is very moved by the integration of her notion of God. Now she is able to turn to Jesus.

Andrea to Jesus: "I am now ready to accept you as the masculine channel of God and accept you into my heart." Andrea is happy and accepts both Jesus and Mary Magdalene into her heart. She can feel the love that connects the two and that can now flow into her.

Andrea to John: "Thank you for bringing me closer to Jesus. I allow myself to find my own path to Jesus."

Feedback one month later
Andrea calls to tell me that she has successfully let go of her ex-boyfriend, John. She now feels complete and no longer needs to project her male divine channel onto John.

CASE 24

"Things can't go well for me" - blocked joy for life

Individual constellation

Mandy F. is married and has three children

Mandy comes to my office with the following symptoms: swollen abdomen, stomach pressure and an enlarged liver. Mandy: "I've always got some sort of pain. I'd love to feel good, function normally and treat my body better. As soon as I start feeling better, I stop caring for myself. I'd like to analyze and resolve the psychological causes for my physical symptoms so that that I can enjoy a pain-free life."

Individual constellation with pillows
Mandy places a pillow for herself, one for her goal (the ability to feel good and enjoy life) and one for the impediment.

Perception at Mandy's position: "I squint at the blockage and sense that I can feel a little better, but not too much. Behind this blockage I see the Catholic Church and many men to whom I relinquished my power and strength as a woman. I feel small and at their mercy. They impose many restrictions and intimidate me."

I ask Mandy to take her own place and speak the following resolution statements:

Resolution statements to resolve this and previous lives
Mandy to the Catholic Church: "I now take back all of the power and strength that I relinquished to you." She takes this energy directly into her solar plexus and feels stronger. Her fears fade away and she perceives herself as an equal.

"I relinquish all your commandments and restrictions; they no longer serve me. I release myself from the notion that physical pleasure is something bad, that life is for suffering as an ascetic and that one must bear a cross in life in order to enter heaven. I dissolve the concept that life is the fall of mankind for which I must punish myself.
I take leave of the church's guilt and atonement program and accept responsibility for having chosen to live and learn from my experiences. I retract my vows as a nun and priest in former lives to love only God and release myself from my vows of chastity, to refrain from physical and worldly pleasures. I am grateful for all of my learning experiences with the Catholic Church. I now consider it good between us. I am prepared to fully and completely enjoy my body, desire and sexuality."

Mandy feels deeply moved and relieved after speaking the resolution statements. I suggest that she now reintegrate the facet of her femininity that was severed during her former lives.

Resolution statements to reintegrate disassociated facets
Mandy to herself: "I now take back the promise I made not to use my power of vision and allow myself to live my life to the fullest and as it best fits my needs. I release myself from the promise never again to heal and take back all of my healing abilities, my knowledge and wisdom. I am free from the promise never to speak the truth about myself and allow myself to express the full truth and intuitions I perceive."

Now an integrated whole, Mandy seems able to achieve her goal of feeling good and enjoying her life. Mandy: It feels like cleansing water is flowing over me, blessing and fulfilling me." She describes it as a divine moment that she's never experienced before. She now feels the need to express gratitude for her life to her mother, who died during childbirth.

Mandy to her mother: "Dear mother, thank you for my life. I will now enjoy it to the fullest in your honor. Please give me your blessing, that I may be successful in this quest."

Feedback one year later
Mandy: "Although I had some difficult times in the past year, I'm thankful for all of the doors that have opened as a result of my development. I now feel joy

and pleasure in life and treat myself more lovingly. My spirituality has opened my awareness and I feel confident that I have everything I need in life. I've begun making my world a more positive place. I still have pain, but I'm working with physical therapy methods."

CASE 25

Pregnancy and sexuality – the lethal threat

Individual constellation

Maria R. is 32 years old, married and does not yet have children

Maria comes to me for an individual session. She is pregnant for the first time and is excited about the baby. Maria: "Ever since I became pregnant it doesn't feel right to have sex with my husband. It's like I don't even notice he's there; all of my attention is focused on my baby. It's been several weeks since we had sex. I'm afraid that if I continue rejecting his sexual advances that he'll find someone else to satisfy his needs. I'd like to know why I'm not open to sex during the pregnancy.

Individual constellation with blocks
Maria places a red block for herself, a blue one for the baby next to her and a green one for her husband a short distance away opposite the other two. In this constellation, her baby takes the partner position to her right side, whereas her husband is excluded from the mother-child relationship. I ask Maria to place another block for the reason why her husband is excluded from her relationship with the child. She takes a large red block and places it between herself and her husband. In this block I see one of Maria's previous lives as a prostitute.

Maria as a prostitute in a previous life
The image shows Maria impregnated by her former partner, who was her pimp. She contracted syphilis during her pregnancy due to unprotected intercourse with him and died with the baby in her womb. The last impression from that life was equating sex with her partner with death for her and her baby! Maria is shocked by the images and finds it difficult to forgive her former partner for what happened.

Effects on Maria's current life
Because Maria still carries this negative impression, she still perceives sexuality during pregnancy as a lethal threat for herself and her baby.

109

Resolution statements to resolve this previous life
Maria feels like her partner's victim in this former life. The key is to recognize that she carries some share in the blame for having unsafe sex with a sexually promiscuous man.

<u>Maria to her former partner</u>: "You must bear your share in the blame for our deaths. I also accept my share of the responsibility for my foolish actions, which put me and my baby in danger."

I ask Maria to accept the pregnant woman she used to be and to give her a feeling of safety and security. While doing so, tears stream down her cheeks. She should imagine letting go of the old impression that "sex with a man means death for me and my baby."

Constellation picture
Maria looks again at the block constellation and sees that her current partner poses absolutely no threat to her and her baby. He has no sexual relations with other women and looks forward to having a child together. She now feels able to be physically open to him without hesitation. She and the baby are now safe.

Resolution statements to resolve the roles
<u>Maria to her husband:</u> "Dear Ralph, you are my partner, not our baby."
<u>Maria to her baby:</u> "You are not my partner, you are our child and your father is my partner."
Her husband now stands on her right side and their baby close to both of them.

Feedback two weeks later
Maria calls to thank me. She's happy that she can now enjoy sex with her husband and looks forward to their new family.

CASE 26

Unfulfilled wish for children

"Dear great-grandmother, I honor the loss of your four children" – Unfulfilled wish for children

Group constellation

Mary L. is 32 years old, Anthony L. is 34 years old; they are married and have no children

Mary and Anthony have already tried artificial insemination twice. Mary got pregnant the second time, but lost the baby after four weeks. A friend recommended a family constellation session before their third attempt. During the preliminary meeting they disclose that several people in both of their families had died young. I recommend that they first constellate their ancestral families.

Mary's ancestral family constellation
Initially her representative cannot deal with the issue of having children, since she is stuck in the place of several ancestors who died young. She is therefore unable to focus on her own life and start her own family. She feels too strained to take on new responsibility as a mother.

Resolution statements
Mary to her ancestors who died young: "You are part of the family. I honor and respect your destiny and your premature deaths. You have your own place, which I cannot take. Please look kindly upon me, so that I may live a good life." Her ancestors look kindly on Mary and bless her. Mary's maternal great-grandmother lost four children during childbirth. From her she acquired a fear of giving birth to additional children for fear of losing another.

Mary to her great-grandmother: "Dear great-grandma, I honor your difficult fate and the loss of your four children." Mary bows before her. "I give up your feelings of sadness and guilt. I also lovingly relinquish your fear of conceiving another child for fear they may also perish. You experienced and suffered through this, not me. Please bless me so that my children may come into this life strong and healthy. I thank you." Mary is very moved while speaking these resolution statements.

Mary substitutes for her parents' mothers and is therefore bound in her responsibility for her parents. She relinquishes this responsibility to her parents and grandparents in order to take her place as their child. After these entanglements have been resolved, she feels like a heavy burden has been removed and she can focus on her own life. Mary accepts her great-grandmother's blessing for children. Her parents now stand behind her and bless her fertility. As a first step, we let the healing images from the constellation sink in.

CASE 27

Unfulfilled wish for children

"I'm responsible for your death" – a previous life as a babysitter

Individual session

Continuation of Case 26
Two weeks after the ancestral family constellation, Mary and Anthony come to me for an individual session. Mary tells me about a regression she'd done two months ago because of inexplicable feelings of sadness. My testing shows that her old trauma is still present, so I ask her to tell her story.

Mary's previous life as a babysitter – I'm to blame for your death!
Mary: "I saw myself as a babysitter of two children, a boy and a girl aged 2 and 5. They were both very close to me, like my own children. When I looked away for just a moment, both were killed in an accident. I couldn't see how they died, but I know that it was my fault for not paying enough attention. I test and see that Mary still carries strong feelings of guilt from this life that bar her from becoming a mother.

Resolution statements to resolve Maria's previous life
Mary to the children: "Dear children, I accept my part of the responsibility for not having watched you more closely. I am so sorry! (Mary cries as she says this). I now leave you with your decision to leave this life. You were like my own children and you will always have a special place in my heart. I leave you with your parents, who are responsible for you and hold you in their hearts." Both children's souls look kindly on Mary and her desire to have children. Mary seems relieved and I do not detect any feelings of guilt in her. It appears that one of the children from former times wants to incarnate as her child. Mary is very excited about this.

Anthony also tells me about a regression that led him to a life among the Mayas. In him as well I detect a trauma that needs to be resolved. He describes the following images to me:

Anthony as a Maya priest in a previous life – children must be sacrificed to the gods

Anthony: "I only saw a white screen, but the regression therapist saw me as a Mayan priest. She saw how I continually sacrificed people to the gods. It was a brutal ritual. Many children were also among those sacrificed." Anthony is deeply affected by this and his face contorts. I test and see that he still feels guilty towards the children and bears a strong feeling of responsibility. This blocks him from having children to this today.

Resolution statements to resolve Anthony's previous life

Anthony to the former gods, in whom he believed: "I now accept my part of the responsibility for what I did. I relinquish your responsibility in requiring human sacrifices from me. I now disassociate myself from the notion that God requires human sacrifice. This belief no longer serves me."

Anthony to the sacrificed children: "I'm sorry for what I did at the time and I accept my part of the responsibility for my actions. I now leave you with your responsibility for the victim's role, which you chose as a learning experience." Anthony feels like he's been absolved from a heavy burden. My testing shows no more feelings of guilt.

Feedback eight months later

Mary tells me that she'd become pregnant in the meanwhile, but that she lost the baby again. They will be going on holiday soon to take a mental break from their attempts to have children. Afterwards they will start again with artificial insemination. Since testing shows constellation work cannot help them further with having children, I recommend seeing a good physical therapist who in the past was able to help many couples experiencing difficulty having children.

CASE 28

Unfulfilled wish for children

Hormone deficiency – feelings of guilt from a previous life

Remote constellation

Janet K. is 39 years old, in a relationship and has no children

Janet and her boyfriend have been trying for a baby for three years. She explains on the phone that she often has the feeling of being pregnant, but that the fertilized egg keeps getting rejected. Doctors performed a hormone analysis which showed low levels of progesterone, which may be age-related. This hormone is responsible for the fertilized egg's nidation in the uterine lining, among other things. She's recently begun taking hormone supplements to make up for this deficiency. She asks me to check for psychological reasons for this progesterone deficiency and rejection of the egg. I'm anxious to see if the constellation can grant insight into this matter.

Remote constellation with blocks
I place a figure representing Janet, a red block for her desire for children and a yellow one for her progesterone production. As soon as I place the yellow block, I see images from a previous life:

Janet as a queen in a former life
I see that Janet was once a queen who was unable to have children due to infertility. Because she was jealous of other women's ability to conceive, she poisoned all of the women in her immediate vicinity to make them infertile as well. Janet still bears strong feelings of guilt because of her former actions, which hinders her attempts to conceive a child.

Resolution statements to resolve her previous life
<u>Janet to the women in her former life:</u> "I'm very sorry for what I did to you. Because of my jealousy I kept you from experiencing the joy of motherhood. I now accept responsibility for my actions. I return your power and dignity as women and mothers and your control over your own bodies. I relinquish your responsibility for choosing to experience that life with me. You are now free to be mothers and I bless your fertility. Please look kindly upon me, that I may now completely accept my fertility and have my own children."

Testing shows that Janet no longer feels guilty towards these women from her former life. Testing also shows an activation of her progesterone production.

Debriefing

I ask Janet to speak the resolution sentences immediately on the telephone. We subsequently ask Saint Mary to bless all of the women who became infertile in this former life. We both feel how much love and healing flows into this old life. I sense that the affected women now look kindly upon Janet and her wish for children. She will continue taking her progesterone supplement to ensure sufficient hormone levels.

Feedback seven months later

Janet calls and excitedly tells me that she's in her fourth month of pregnancy. She's very happy that it finally worked and thanks me for my support. I'm glad to hear the good news and wish all the best for her and her baby.

CASE 29

Unfulfilled desire for children

Folic acid deficiency – forbidden love as a nun

Individual constellation

Andrea F. is 36 years old, married and has no children

Andrea comes to me for an individual session. She wants to have a baby together with her husband, but it just doesn't seem to work out. Kinesiologic testing shows that Andrea has a folic acid deficiency. She assures me that she takes sufficient folic acid and knows that it's important for a successful pregnancy. Further testing shows me that Andrea's cells cannot absorb the folic acid from her nutritional supplements. We constellate this blockade with blocks.

Individual constellation with blocks

Andrea chooses a blue figure for herself and a red block for the blockage hindering her cells from absorbing the folic acid. When I look at the red block, I see images from one of Andrea's previous lives as a nun in an abbey.

Andrea as a nun in a previous life

The picture shows Andrea as a young nun and the Reverend Mother as her present mother-in-law. Both were in love with the abbot, who is Andrea's present husband. He only had eyes for the young nun. They had an intimate relationship and she became pregnant by him. As soon as the Reverend Mother discovered this, she accused Andrea of seducing the abbot and threw her out of the abbey. The blame and responsibility was placed solely on her; the abbot was allowed to stay in the abbey.

Consequences for Andrea's current life
These old feelings of guilt hinder Andrea from becoming pregnant with her husband (the former abbot) today. She lacks inner permission to have and raise a child together with him. This results in a physical inability to absorb folic acid and thus subconsciously prevents her pregnancy.

Resolution statements to resolve this previous life
<u>Andrea to her former Reverend Mother (present mother-in-law):</u> "I'm sorry that you suffered as a result of our love, because you also loved him. I am not responsible for his choosing to love me and not you. What went on between you has nothing to do with me. I am not solely responsible for what happened. I accept my part of the responsibility for my actions and leave yours with you. I now take back my power, strength and dignity as a woman and mother as well as the freedom to choose when and with whom I will have children. I absolve these feelings of guilt."

<u>Andrea to the former abbot (today her husband):</u> "I accept my share of the blame and responsibility for our relationship and the resulting pregnancy and relinquish your share. Even though our love was forbidden back then, today I allow you to be my partner and the father of our children."

Andrea lets out a big sigh of relief. Andrea: "Now I know why I felt aggression towards my mother-in-law during recent visits. I had no idea where it came from. We normally get along very well, but somehow I must have sensed that she was blocking us from having children."

Subsequent testing shows that Andrea has released all of these old feelings of guilt. Her present mother-in-law will also grant her blessing that Andrea may have a son together with her son.
Testing for folic acid absorption now shows positive results.

Feedback five months later
I call Andrea to ask how things are going with getting pregnant.
Andrea: "I haven't called you yet, because we haven't officially told anyone. I'm in my third month of pregnancy and hope everything turns out well! We are so looking forward to our baby! Thank you for your help and I believe that it really did work."

I wish Andrea all the best for her pregnancy and that she may soon hold her baby in her arms.

ANIMAL CONSTELLATIONS

I will only briefly touch on animal constellations in this book. With respect to reincarnation I believe that animals have also lived multiple lives. I have not specialized in animals' former lives, but testing on my own dog showed that he has already been a cat and is now incarnated as a dog for the second time. Those who have a cat, dog or other pet can affirm that an animal is a true family member. They are part of the family dynamic and like everything else in a common household are affected by both positive and negative events. It is widely known that children are especially sensitive carriers of energy. They often have difficulty distancing themselves from conflicts between their parents or other key people. They emotionally internalize much that isn't physically manifested. In my constellation work, I often see how children burden themselves with much of their parents' feelings of anger, sadness, disappointment, etc.

Many symptoms of illness in children can be resolved by working with the parents or other family members. The same is true for pets. They also acquire unresolved conflicts and feelings from their owners. I have done several animal constellations and have experienced how a dog bore his owner's longing for death and subsequently died in an accident. In a friend's constellation, it became clear that his cat had acquired his kidney illness. Animals relieve the strain on their owners much as children for their parents. Constellations with animals clearly show their role in the family. Sometimes pets take on the role of the long-awaited child that has not yet come. Sometimes they are identified with an aborted child that was mourned too little and taken to heart. Often a pet takes the place of a spouse from a first marriage who has not yet received their esteemed position in the family system. Sometimes pets are a substitute for a partner. Animals reflect many of our moods and feelings; there is seldom a happy dog alongside a depressed owner. Even if the dog cheers up its sad owner, then the dog is also taking away some of the sadness. Even relationship conflicts are often acquired and exhibited by our pets. Here's an example:

CASE 30

My dog's enteritis – anger towards my husband

Individual constellation

Sabina K. is 36 years old, married, pregnant and has a dog named Belle.

Sabina comes to me and explains the following issue: "My dog Belle has been acting so strange for the last two weeks! She's ill-tempered, restless, doesn't obey my commands and eats very little. When my husband, Peter, comes home from work, she's normally very excited and greets him. Now she seems very reserved around him. The veterinarian said that Bella has enteritis, which we're treating with tablets. However, a good friend of mine recommended that I do a constellation for Belle to see if psychosomatic causes could be responsible for the infection.

Individual constellation with blocks

Since animals often assume their owner's issues, I ask Sabine to choose three blocks – one for Belle, one her herself and one for her husband. Sabine places herself and Peter some distance apart and chooses a red block for Belle, placing it near herself. My perception in Belle's position is of aggression and resentment. Testing shows that these are not Belle's own feelings. The anger is Sabine's and it is directed towards her husband, Peter. When I ask Sabine what makes her angry about Peter, she thinks for a moment and replies, "Yes, I can think of something. I recently became pregnant. It's our first child and we're very happy about it. The thing is, since I've been pregnant, Peter hasn't been sexually interested in me at all. He only sees the mother in me and not the attractive woman I always was to him. That makes me angry!" Sabine's story now explains why Belle no longer greets her master as usual. She is expressing Sabina's frustration. Her ill temper now also makes sense to Sabina.

Resolution statements

I suggest that Sabine become aware of and accept her anger with Peter. Half the solution lies in recognizing her feelings. I also recommend that she speak with Peter about this in order to find a common solution for the sexual blockade. If Peter wants, he can also work together with me on a constellation. To free Belle from Sabina's feelings, I ask Sabina to speak the following resolution statements:

Resolution statements

<u>Sabine to her dog, Belle:</u> "Dear Belle, I now take back my frustration and anger towards Peter; you are free. Even when I have conflicts with your master, you may still be happy to be near him." Sabine is relieved at having removed the burden from Belle. She's happy to talk about this lack of sexuality with Peter and to find a solution together with him. Subsequent testing shows and there are no more burdens weighing on Belle.

Call from Peter

After a talk with Sabina about our constellation, Peter calls me in the evening and asks me to perform a remote constellation for him. Peter: "I don't really know how I should approach Sabina sexually. I now see her only as the mother of our child and it somehow seems taboo to sleep with her. It's like my desire's been put on ice!"

Remote constellation with blocks
I position Peter, Sabina and Peter's parents and see the following picture. Peter's feeling that he cannot have sex with a pregnant woman has been acquired from his father, who considered it taboo to desire and sleep with a pregnant woman. I give Peter the following resolution statements on the telephone:

Resolution statements
Peter to his father: "Dear dad, I now lovingly release your belief that a man cannot sleep with a pregnant woman. Please look kindly upon me for having a happy sex life with Sabina during her pregnancy, even if you were unable to do so." Peter confirms later on the phone that he perceived his parent's sexuality as very taboo. Peter: "We never talked about it. I can imagine that my father often drank away his sex drive with alcohol."

Feedback one week later
Sabina calls and tells me that Belle is back to normal. Sabine: "She seems carefree, eats normally and is happy when Peter comes home from work. Our sex life is now slowly developing again. I'm very happy that we did the constellation. It helped us resolve a lot of issues."

This is just one of many cases with animal constellations. Since I know how much pet owners love their pets, I can fully recommend doing a constellation for your furry friends if necessary. You can test in advance if your pet is carrying a burden for you. I also do many animal constellations remotely.

That, which is meant to touch the heart, must come from the heart.

Johann Wolfgang von Goethe, Faust II

HEALING IMAGES

A healing image is the final stage of a constellation that leads to the goal or desired result. A classical healing image in your ancestral family ensures that you have your own good place in the family constellation, are free of external entanglements and grants you freedom over your own life with based on the strength of your ancestors.

Good resolutions in a constellation
A good resolution comes primarily when the client is ready for it. Every entanglement and blockage acquired from the family system serves for development and must be resolved in its own time. A resolution presupposes that the associated learning process has been completed. Only then can a good resolution come about. Very often it proves difficult to relinquish an assumed responsibility and finally be free for your own life. Those who are accustomed to bearing others' burdens find themselves continually stuck in the same rut. It feels suddenly empty and uncluttered to no longer carry burdens and be able to concentrate on one's own needs in life. In this case, it is helpful to have a companion after the constellation to help you navigate this newfound freedom and find your purpose in life. As long as my grandmother's anger towards men serves me in not having to enter into a relationship, then I will not want to relinquish these feelings.

Former lives as a blockade in a constellation
I have had to interrupt some ancestral constellations because we approached an issue that could not be resolved despite all efforts. Very often these are blockades from former lives that must be resolved first. Only afterwards can order be returned to the family system. Although I work with images from former lives, I am not always able to resolve these karmic entanglements, especially when the issue is very complex. In this case, it has proved helpful to analyze these issues individually with a spiritual reading or regression.

A partial resolution as a good resolution
Very often people have the illusion that you can do an ancestral constellation once and resolve all entanglements, allowing the parents to be lovingly accepted into one's heart. A lot of preparatory work is required for this. Not all of our issues are ready to be resolved at the same time. A step-by-step constellation is then a good alternative. For example, one can easily resolve the mother's side even though the father's side is not yet ready.

We can only resolve what our soul reveals
I experience time and again that the constellation of a specific issue unexpectedly turns into another issue. This is due to the fact that each constellation represents

an image from our soul. When Bert Hellinger speaks of "movements of the soul," this is the best expression of what we see in a constellation. We are led by our minds and therefore amass certain desired results for our lives, but subconsciously we are preoccupied with completely different issues which must be resolved first. If we trustingly open ourselves to these images from the soul, these can lead us to unexpected solutions. These may not correspond exactly to what we've initially imagined, but it could be the next step in finding the final solution to our issue. Often a constellation reveals a difficult issue such as murder, rape, war trauma, fleeing from our homes or bitter poverty. Such issues burden our ancestral system and thus also the constellator so much that it moves to the center in order to be resolved first.

Images from the soul cannot be comprehended with reason
Not all of the images in a constellation can immediately be processed by our reason. I have often received feedback saying that images from the constellation do not completely coincide with reality. They only make sense when you consider why an image is revealed in a certain manner during a constellation. Sometimes these are images from former lives that become visible in the constellation. Sometimes they are symbolic representations which must be interpreted first, like dreams. For this reason, we cannot take images from the soul revealed in a constellation and relate them one-to-one with our reality; it is beyond the grasp of our reason.

Accepting our parents into our hearts
One of the most beautiful and desirable healing images is when a client hugs accepts their parents into their hearts. Not only is this vital for our own ability to lead a happy relationship, but we also hug ourselves in the process. We are our parents in that we carry their personality facets in ourselves.

Only by accepting our parents' personality facets in ourselves can we realize our own potential.

Accepting our parents in the constellations is sometimes difficult because of unresolved childhood injuries connected with anger or sadness. Healing our inner child is therefore a prerequisite for accepting our parents. This healing work leads us away from placing blame and towards taking responsibility for loving ourselves (see "The Inner Child in Us"). If we lack the humility necessary to accept our parents' strengths and weaknesses and believe we can do everything better, then it will be difficult to graciously accept them and the life they've granted us. Our parents' lives can only be viewed as a whole, without exceptions.

We can't pick out the bad, but have to recognize every personality facet even if we'd rather not identify with it. "Mom, I'll never be like you" always leads to repetition or becomes a shadow facet that is always projected onto others. What I disassociate myself from will always be reflected in my surroundings (see Shadow facets). Usually there are also karmic entanglements with our parents from former lives that must be resolved before we can accept them into our hearts. Work with our parents is like an onion, in that there are many different layers. This can rarely be achieved with a single constellation. However, there is also a good resolution in being able to integrate one's parents bit by bit.

The complexity of a healing image

Besides many other issues, most of my clients want a more fulfilling relationship and family, career development and good income. These are very complex issues that can seldom be resolved in one constellation session or without additional aid from other forms of therapy. Constellation work forms the basis for all of these issues. In my form of integrative family constellation, I also consider negative impressions, inner child injuries and karmic entanglements n in my constellation work in order to reach a more comprehensive resolution.

Effect of a healing image

A question I repeatedly get is how and when a healing image from in a constellation will take effect in this life? In many of my constellations, the effect is immediate.

Example

Irene has been trying unsuccessfully to sell her house for a long time. She does a group constellation with me and resolves the associated blockades. She goes home, opens the door, the phone rings and she's found a buyer for her house. I usually get very positive feedback about how quickly family behavioral patterns change, how suddenly closeness and love becomes possible or how communication breakdowns quickly reside.

If a healing image can't be found, then the client is either not ready for it or has not yet taken an important step towards a good resolution. During the debriefings I can usually determine what is required in order to reach the desired goal. Complex issues can only be resolved like the layers of an onion. Sometimes constellation work alone is sufficient; others may need other helpful methods to break down these blockades. A good complement to constellation has proved to be the kinesiologic separation of childhood injuries or traumatic experiences from former lives. Spiritual readings can resolve causal blockades in present and former lives by reading our bodies' own energy fields. There are many other possibilities to heal an issue in its complexity. The sum of many things creates the whole. I therefore enjoy working with a network of therapists, psychologists and energy consultants because this cooperation is more effective in resolving complex issues than one method alone. Even if the entire wish cannot immediately be realized, then partial resolutions are always a crucial step in helping the constellator on their journey.

Just like the enchanted figures in fairy tales - they are all awoken at the right time.

QUESTIONS AND ANSWERS

Which constellation form is best?
The constellation form you'll want to use depends on the issue to be resolved as well as your personal preference. With regard to success, all three methods work equally well. I can usually determine in the preliminary talks which constellation best fits the wishes and needs of the constellator.

Group constellations
One advantage of group constellations is the ability to directly experience the representatives and their relationships to one another. Important figures such as parents, grandparents and siblings can be hugged as gestures of belonging and sympathy by the constellator. It can be very emotionally moving and healing to take part in this group process.

Individual constellation
Individual sessions have become much more common. Increasingly more people are taking part in these, particularly those who are not keen to share their problems with a group. I use pillows or blocks as representatives in this case. I normally place myself in the various positions in order to perceive with whom my client is entangled. Pillows enable the constellator to take the position of a family member in order to perceive an image from their perspective. This allows the individual to better understand and perceive their own situation. The advantage of constellations with blocks is that you can summarize the entire group dynamic on the meta-level. You can maintain a clear overview even in constellations with multiple representatives. Perceptions in pillows or blocks, which represent a certain person, also allow the constellator's feelings to flow and can bring their experiences with difficult fates to the fore. All of the entanglements are subsequently taken into account with the resolution statements.

Remote constellation
This is a new method I've developed and use very often. It is practical in cases where people live far away from me or when working together on-site is difficult. Remote constellations are comfortable and save time for the constellator because there is no travel involved. This method has also proved useful for quick constellations regarding urgent issues. I primarily use blocks in remote constellations to create a good overview for myself. When I perceive the different blocks, I experience how the respective person feels and what they need. I also see many images from present and former lives. I then formulate the entire healing resolution and give my clients the required resolution statements per phone or email, which the constellator then speaks at home or directly on the telephone.

Which information must I provide for the constellation?
The basis of every constellation is always the ancestral family. Who has been excluded or forgotten (e.g. those who died young) in your family system as has not received a secure place? It is best to create a family genogram first (see Glossary). Your ancestors' difficult situations, e.g. being forced to flee their homes, war trauma, violence, etc., are important.

The preliminary information necessary for a constellation also depends on the issue to be resolved. This will be discussed in detail during the preliminary talk.

I am adopted and have no information about my biological ancestral family. Can I still do a constellation?
I have already done many constellations for clients who were adopted (see Case 8). The most important entanglements are revealed in the constellation picture, even without any prior information. Besides that, I also do kinesiologic testing for many burdens. Furthermore, you can never know everything about your ancestors; family secrets are revealed in every third or fourth constellation.

Is my anonymity guaranteed in a constellation?
As a trained life coach and social counselor, I am bound by professional discretion. People are only introduced by their first names in group constellations. In the best interest of all participants, a codex is agreed upon prior to the constellation in which everything that happens during the constellation will not be mentioned to outside of the constellation. From my personal experience, I can confirm that the participants very strictly adhere to this agreement. In individual and remote constellations there are no third-party representatives. You communicate only with me as a coach.

Does it suffice to speak the resolution statements once or do I have to repeat them multiple times?
It is usually sufficient to speak the resolution statements once in order to achieve the desired effect. For difficult entanglements it has proven useful to repeat the resolution statements several times in order to anchor them deeply.

Can you speak about a constellation after it's been done or does this negate the effect?
It's better not to speak about the constellation for a couple of days, as otherwise you risk skewing it before it has taken effect. The healing resolution should be well integrated before you speak about it. When you attempt to comprehend what has happened step by step in your head, then you move away from the healing resolution that has begun to take effect. It's best to let it go and wait for the effects. The constellation will work in any case, whether or not you speak about it. If speaking about it is necessary to process it, then it's best to do so with the constellation practitioner.

Do I need follow-up support after a constellation?
Sometimes aspects arise after a constellation that must still be resolved. Subsequent support can be very important in order to gain strength when moving from old to new life structures. I always offer follow-up consultations and the client can choose whether or not they partake in them.

How often may I constellate my family?
Some are of the opinion that one should only constellate their ancestral family once; I personally do not ascribe to this belief. You can seldom complete the entire family system with one constellation. I see working with the family as an onion layer process. Resolving individual issues from your father's or mother's side of the family come at their own time; they can only be resolved when they're ready. That's why different aspects arise at various times during a constellation.

Do former lives appear in every constellation?
Images from the constellation determine the necessity of including previous lives. It usually happens unexpectedly. About one-third of my constellations are connected with issues from past lives.

Can I also work with past lives even if I don't believe to have previously lived?
Many of my clients are not prepared to work with images from past lives. When these appear, they are surprised. Several have never thought about the possibility of have lived in former times. When I recently asked a client if he believed in previous lives, he answered, "It's a nice idea that life continues after death." Even people who do not believe in former lives can usually easily accept the images that I see. This is probably due to the fact that they find a certain resonance in what I tell them. It suffices to accept the necessary resolution statements, after which they can begin working.

Love is the ultimate purpose in the history of the world, the amen of the universe.

Novalis, fragments

AFTERWORD

All those who've personally experienced a family constellation will agree with me that you can't really describe this process in words. Tears when the love begins to flow again, the first time to completely accept your parents into your heart or to finally take your own place in life: all of these are deeply moving experiences that can come about in a constellation. Many of my clients have realized their dreams of resolving entanglements and negative beliefs. To experience this personally is the greatest reward and gives me the most energy for my work. Perhaps my book has inspired you also to find out in which ancestral line you or your family members have already been incarnated. You'll gain a completely new understanding of your current life through this realization. If you are a consultant, therapist or psychologist, then I hope to have enriched your work just a little bit with my methods.

Glossary

Age of Aquarius: an astronomical epoch often viewed as a new beginning in the spiritual evolution of humans.

Ancestors: female or male predecessors.

Ancestral family: lineage. For a list of those who belong in an ancestral family constellation, see family genogram.

Black magic: magic performed with evil intentions. Practitioners of black magic call on supernatural dark powers – devils, demons and evil sprits – and conduct ceremonies in which malignant powers are conjured to inflict damage upon others.

Buddhism: is an Indian / East Asian philosophy founded by Buddha. Among other things, Buddhism deals with karma, the positive or negative consequences of our behavior on this or future lives, as well as with the causes of reincarnation.

Buddhist: a follower of Buddhism.

Chakra: aural energy centers in human beings.

Channeling: opening channels for messages from the spiritual world.

Codex: this term applies to an agreement made by a group in a family constellation. It mostly governs the privacy of what takes place in the constellation, that it will not be shared outside of the constellation.

Collective guilt: a collective is a group of people who live together in which the individual's personality is given a lower priority. Collective guilt is the guilt of a whole group.

Dissociated facets: personality facets which are not integrated.

Dynamics: an area of mechanics that focuses on the active forces in the movement sequences of bodies.

Emotion: state of feeling.

Energetics: a philosophy based on the idea that energy is the constitution and fundamental force of all things.

Energy practitioner: follower of the philosophy of energetics.

Family genogram: a compilation of both maternal and paternal ancestors up to five generations. Among these are: myself and my siblings (those living as well as dead e.g. through abortion, death or miscarriage), my parents and their siblings, my grandparents and their siblings, my great-grandparents and their siblings and perhaps my great-great-grandparents as well. The following are also a part: former spouses, fiancées and perhaps an ancestor's first great love.

Feng Shui: is the art and science of living in harmony with one's surroundings.

Hinduism: religion found primarily in India. One of the core tenets of Hinduism is that a person's positive or negative actions create karma and have consequences for future incarnations.

Humility: the ability to bow before greater powers, such as God or the difficult fates of our ancestors.

Identification: in family constellation, this means that when one represents an ancestor; one remembers them and identifies with this person and their fate.

Incarnation: the assumption that mind and soul are substantiate.

Integration-integrative: instauration, accepting disassociated facets into our personality for healing and to become complete.

Intuition: ideas, feelings and perceptions that cannot be explained logically.

Karma: the law of cause and effect; you reap what you sow. Hindus are convinced that a person's present living situations are the result of their actions in former lives.

Kinesiology: the science of human movement in the broadest sense. Applied kinesiology deals with muscles and forms a bridge to energy systems in Chinese acupuncture studies.

Mandala: is Sanskrit for circle. In Hinduism and to some extent in Buddhism it is a symbol of the universe used as an aid in meditation. The mandalas, variously interpreted as symbols of completeness and unity or as a depiction of the sun, can be compared with "passageways" to the inner sanctum.

Magic (magical/black magic/white magic): controlling natural powers and spirits with secret means or symbolic actions; associations with evil powers is black magic, with powers that provide blessings white magic.

Medium: is an intermediary who can perceive and pass on messages from nonphysical entities, such as spirits or the deceased.

Mental bodies: our physical body is surrounded by many aural bodies, one of which is our mental body. It contains all of the mental contents of our lives, such as beliefs that we carry from this or former lives.

Meta level: a meta level is a superordinate level or perception that allows for distance in an observation.

Polarity: the existence of two poles, opposites, that is often used in reincarnation therapy because of the need to accept victim-perpetrator roles, good and evil, light and darkness, love and hate, etc.

Present family: among one's present family is the constellator themselves, their partner, common children, former spouses and common children, fiancées and perhaps a great love.

Projection: rejection, a defense mechanism of unfavorable, forbidden or unwanted notions, needs, desires and feelings that are shifted onto other people in order to reject and fight them there.

Psychology: the science of mental processes.

Reading: the reading of images and information from our own physical energyfield.

Regression: mental regression to our childhood or a former life.

Reincarnation: rebirth, resurrection; the assumption that after death a soul can materialize in other physical bodies.

Self-identity – Identity: the inner unit of a person experienced as "oneself".

Shadow facets: repressed personality facets which we are not fond of.

Somatic: physical.

Soul: the term soul has different meanings in various contexts. In philosophy, a soul is understood to be a mental principle that gives life. In psychology it is the conceptual aggregation of humans' experiencing, feeling and acting. In religion, a soul is understood as the part of a higher being that, in contrast to our bodies, is immortal.
Transmigration: the belief that a human soul can pass to another human or animal body at death up to complete catharsis.

Subconscious: various experiences are subconsciously stored in us and are not easily accessible by our consciousness. When we dream, we have a strong connection with our subconscious.

Systemic: a system is an order that is organized or constructed according to something specific. In family constellation, we assume that family members are connected with one another according to certain laws or systems. Each disruption of the system has negative consequences.

Therapist: a therapist is a practitioner of therapeutic procedures.

Transformation: alteration, conversion.

Trauma: mental or physical shock, serious mental or physical ordeals.

Vows: a strict oath made before God.

BIBLIOGRAPHY

Arminger, M., Das innere Kind. Heyne, 1993
Bradshow, J., Das Kind in uns. Knaur, 2000
Chopich, J. E., Aussöhnung mit dem inneren Kind. Ullstein, 1999
Detlefsen, T. und Dahlke,E., Krankheit als Weg. C. Bertelsmann, 1983
Detlefsen, T., Schicksal als Chance. Goldmann, 1979
Detlefsen,T., Das Erlebnis der Wiedergeburt. Goldmann, 1976
Drury, N., Lexikon des esoterischen Wissens. Schirner, 2005
Gibran, K., Der Prophet. Walter Verlag, 1991
Grochowiak K., Stresius K. u. Castella J.: NLP & das Familien Stellen, Junfermann, 2001
Harenberg., Lexikon der Sprichwörter & Zitate, Harenberg, 2002
Harris, A. u. T., Einmal o.k. immer o.k., Rowohlt, 1985
Hellinger, B., Ordnungen der Liebe, Carl Auer, 1995
Hellinger, B., Finden was wirkt. Kösel, 1993
Hellinger, B., Entlassen werden wir vollendet, Kösel, 2001
Hellinger, B., Die Quelle braucht nicht nach dem Weg zu fragen, Carl Auer, 2001
Jasmuheen, In Resonanz, Koha, 1998
Kenyon, Tom & Sion J., Das Manuskript der Magdalena, Koha, 2002
Krystal, P, Die Fesseln des Karma sprengen. Ullstein, 2004
Magli, 1., Die Madonna, Pipa, 1987
Mayer, N.Dr., Der Kainkomplex. Zur Zeit leider nicht erhältlich
Mehringer Sell, 1., Mama, glaub mir, ich habe schon einmal gelebt. Schirner 1997
Meyer, H., Die Gesetze des Schicksals. Goldmann, 1992
Meyer, H., Jeder bekommt den Partner, den er verdient. Trigon, 1997
Michel, P., Karma und Gnade. Aquamarin, 2002
Newton M., Die Abenteuer der Seelen. Edition Astrodata, 2001
Roberts, J., Individuum und Massenschicksal, Goldmann 1981
Rogoll, R., Nimm dich wie du bist, Herder, 1999
Satir V., Banmen J., Gerber J., Gomori M., Das Satir - Modell, Junfermann, 2000
Schäfer, T., Was die Seele krank macht und was sie heilt, Knaur, 1998
Starbird, M., Die Frau mit dem Alabaster Krug, Allgria, 2005
Trutz, H., Das große Handbuch der Reinkarnation, Silberschnur, 2003
Ulsamer, B., Ohne Wurzeln keine Flügel, Goldmann 1999
Wambach, H., Leben vor dem Leben. Heyne, 1986
Weber, G., Zweierlei Glück. Auer, 1997
Woolger, R., Vergangene Leben heilen. Goldmann, 2006